6/21

The Banking System in Canada Including the Bank of Canada and the "Big Five" Banks

Patrick Sing

The role of the book within our culture is changing. The change is brought on by new ways to acquire & use content, the rapid dissemination of information and real-time peer collaboration on a global scale. Despite these changes one thing is clear--"the book" in it's traditional form continues to play an important role in learning and communication. The book you are holding in your hands utilizes the unique characteristics of the Internet -- relying on web infrastructure and collaborative tools to share and use resources in keeping with the characteristics of the medium (user-created, defying control, etc.)--while maintaining all the convenience and utility of a real book.

Contents

Articles

Introduction **1**

Bank 1

Banking in Canada 18

Early Canadian banking system 24

List of banks and credit unions in Canada 27

British North America Acts 33

Bank of Canada **41**

Bank of Canada 41

Central bank 45

Bank of Canada Building 59

The "Big Five" Banks **61**

Big Five (banks) 61

Royal Bank of Canada 67

Toronto-Dominion Bank 77

Scotiabank 87

Bank of Montreal 94

Canadian Imperial Bank of Commerce 103

Notable Second Tier Banks **119**

National Bank of Canada 119

Desjardins Group 123

HSBC Bank Canada 125

ING Group 129

Regulation

140

Canada Bank Act 140

Office of the Superintendent of Financial Institutions (Canada) 141

Minister of Finance (Canada) 144

Credit union 149

References

Article Sources and Contributors 158

Image Sources, Licenses and Contributors 159

Introduction

Bank

Banking
Types of bank Central bank Advising bank Commercial bank Community development bank Credit union Custodian bank Depository bank German public bank Investment bank Industrial bank Islamic banking Merchant bank Mutual bank Mutual savings bank National bank Offshore bank Private bank Savings bank Swiss bank
Deposit accounts Savings account Transactional account Money market account Time deposit
ATM card Debit card Credit card
Electronic funds transfer Automated Clearing House Electronic bill payment Giro Wire transfer

Banking terms
Anonymous banking
Automatic teller machine
Loan
Money creation
Substitute check
List of banks
Finance series
Financial market
Financial market participants
Corporate finance
Personal finance
Public finance
Banks and Banking
Financial regulation

Finance

A **bank** is a financial intermediary that accepts deposits and channels those deposits into lending activities, either directly or through capital markets. A bank connects customers with capital deficits to customers with capital surpluses.

Banking is generally a highly regulated industry, and government restrictions on financial activities by banks have varied over time and location. The current set of global bank capital standards are called Basel II. In some countries such as Germany, banks have historically owned major stakes in industrial corporations while in other countries such as the United States banks are prohibited from owning non-financial companies. In Japan, banks are usually the nexus of a cross-share holding entity known as the keiretsu. In Iceland banks had very light regulation prior to the 2008 collapse.

The oldest bank still in existence is Monte dei Paschi di Siena, headquartered in Siena, Italy, which has been operating continuously since 1472.

History

Main article: History of banking

Banking in the modern sense of the word can be traced to medieval and early Renaissance Italy, to the rich cities in the north like Florence, Venice and Genoa. The Bardi and Peruzzi families dominated banking in 14th century Florence, establishing branches in many other parts of Europe. Perhaps the most famous Italian bank was the Medici bank, set up by Giovanni Medici in 1397. The earliest known state deposit bank, *Banco di San Giorgio* (Bank of St. George), was founded in 1407 at Genoa, Italy.

Banks can be traced back to ancient times even before money when temples were used to store commodities. During the 3rd century AD, banks in Persia and other territories in the Persian Sassanid Empire issued letters of credit known as *Ṣakks*.[citation needed] Muslim traders are known to have used the cheque or *ṣakk* system since the time of Harun al-Rashid (9th century) of the Abbasid Caliphate. In the 9th century, a Muslim businessman could cash an early form of the cheque in China drawn on sources in Baghdad,Wikipedia:Verifiability a tradition that was significantly strengthened in the 13th and 14th centuries, during the Mongol Empire.[citation needed] Fragments found in the Cairo Geniza indicate that in the 12th century cheques remarkably similar to our own were in use, only smaller to save costs on the paper. They contain a sum to be paid and then the order "May so and so pay the bearer such and such an amount". The date and name of the issuer are also apparent.

Origin of the word

The word *bank* was borrowed in Middle English from Middle French *banque*, from Old Italian *banca*, from Old High German *banc, bank* "bench, counter". Benches were used as desks or exchange counters during the Renaissance by Florentine bankers, who used to make their transactions atop desks covered by green tablecloths.

The earliest evidence of money-changing activity is depicted on a silver Greek drachm coin from ancient Hellenic colony Trapezus on the Black Sea, modern Trabzon, c. 350–325 BC, presented in the British Museum in London. The coin shows a banker's table (*trapeza*) laden with coins, a pun on the name of the city. In fact, even today in Modern Greek the word Trapeza (*Τράπεζα*) means both a table and a bank.

Definition

The definition of a bank varies from country to country. See the relevant country page (below) for more information.

Cathay Bank in Boston's Chinatown.

Under English common law, a banker is defined as a person who carries on the business of banking, which is specified as:

- conducting current accounts for his customers
- paying cheques drawn on him, and
- collecting cheques for his customers.

In most common law jurisdictions there is a Bills of Exchange Act that codifies the law in relation to negotiable instruments, including cheques, and this Act contains a statutory definition of the term *banker*: *banker* includes a body of persons, whether incorporated or not, who carry on the business of banking' (Section 2, Interpretation). Although this definition seems circular, it is actually functional, because it ensures that the legal basis for bank transactions such as cheques does not depend on how the bank is organised or regulated.

The business of banking is in many English common law countries not defined by statute but by common law, the definition above. In other English common law jurisdictions there are statutory definitions of the *business of banking* or *banking business*. When looking at these definitions it is important to keep in mind that they are defining the business of banking for the purposes of the legislation, and not necessarily in general. In particular, most of the definitions are from legislation that has the purposes of entry regulating and supervising banks rather than regulating the actual business of banking. However, in many cases the statutory definition closely mirrors the common law one. Examples of statutory definitions:

- "banking business" means the business of receiving money on current or deposit account, paying and collecting cheques drawn by or paid in by customers, the making of advances to customers, and includes such other business as the Authority may prescribe for the purposes of this Act; (Banking Act (Singapore), Section 2, Interpretation).
- "banking business" means the business of either or both of the following:

1. receiving from the general public money on current, deposit, savings or other similar account repayable on demand or within less than [3 months] ... or with a period of call or notice of less than that period;
2. paying or collecting cheques drawn by or paid in by customers

Since the advent of EFTPOS (Electronic Funds Transfer at Point Of Sale), direct credit, direct debit and internet banking, the cheque has lost its primacy in most banking systems as a payment instrument. This has led legal theorists to suggest that the cheque based definition should be broadened to include financial institutions that conduct current accounts for customers and enable customers to pay and be paid by third parties, even if they do not pay and collect cheques.

Banking

Standard activities

Banks act as payment agents by conducting checking or current accounts for customers, paying cheques drawn by customers on the bank, and collecting cheques deposited to customers' current accounts. Banks also enable customer payments via other payment methods such as telegraphic transfer, EFTPOS, and ATM.

Large door to an old bank vault.

Banks borrow money by accepting funds deposited on current accounts, by accepting term deposits, and by issuing debt securities such as banknotes and bonds. Banks lend money by making advances to customers on current accounts, by making installment loans, and by investing in marketable debt securities and other forms of money lending.

Banks provide almost all payment services, and a bank account is considered indispensable by most businesses, individuals and governments. Non-banks that provide payment services such as remittance companies are not normally considered an adequate substitute for having a bank account.

Banks borrow most funds from households and non-financial businesses, and lend most funds to households and non-financial businesses, but non-bank lenders provide a significant and in many cases adequate substitute for bank loans, and money market funds, cash management trusts and other non-bank financial institutions in many cases provide an adequate substitute to banks for lending savings to.Wikipedia:Please clarify

Channels

Banks offer many different channels to access their banking and other services:

- ATM is a machine that dispenses cash and sometimes takes deposits without the need for a human bank teller. Some ATMs provide additional services.
- A branch is a retail location
- Call center
- Mail: most banks accept check deposits via mail and use mail to communicate to their customers, e.g. by sending out statements
- Mobile banking is a method of using one's mobile phone to conduct banking transactions
- Online banking is a term used for performing transactions, payments etc. over the Internet

- Relationship Managers, mostly for private banking or business banking, often visiting customers at their homes or businesses
- Telephone banking is a service which allows its customers to perform transactions over the telephone without speaking to a human
- Video banking is a term used for performing banking transactions or professional banking consultations via a remote video and audio connection. Video banking can be performed via purpose built banking transaction machines (similar to an Automated teller machine), or via a videoconference enabled bank branch.

Business model

A bank can generate revenue in a variety of different ways including interest, transaction fees and financial advice. The main method is via charging interest on the capital it lends out to customers. The bank profits from the differential between the level of interest it pays for deposits and other sources of funds, and the level of interest it charges in its lending activities.

This difference is referred to as the *spread* between the cost of funds and the loan interest rate. Historically, profitability from lending activities has been cyclical and dependent on the needs and strengths of loan customers and the stage of the economic cycle. Fees and financial advice constitute a more stable revenue stream and banks have therefore placed more emphasis on these revenue lines to smooth their financial performance.

In the past 20 years American banks have taken many measures to ensure that they remain profitable while responding to increasingly changing market conditions. First, this includes the Gramm-Leach-Bliley Act, which allows banks again to merge with investment and insurance houses. Merging banking, investment, and insurance functions allows traditional banks to respond to increasing consumer demands for "one-stop shopping" by enabling cross-selling of products (which, the banks hope, will also increase profitability).

Second, they have expanded the use of risk-based pricing from business lending to consumer lending, which means charging higher interest rates to those customers that are considered to be a higher credit risk and thus increased chance of default on loans. This helps to offset the losses from bad loans, lowers the price of loans to those who have better credit histories, and offers credit products to high risk customers who would otherwise be denied credit.

Third, they have sought to increase the methods of payment processing available to the general public and business clients. These products include debit cards, prepaid cards, smart cards, and credit cards. They make it easier for consumers to conveniently make transactions and smooth their consumption over time (in some countries with underdeveloped financial systems, it is still common to deal strictly in cash, including carrying suitcases filled with cash to purchase a home).

However, with convenience of easy credit, there is also increased risk that consumers will mismanage their financial resources and accumulate excessive debt. Banks make money from card products through interest payments and fees charged to consumers and transaction fees to companies that accept the cards. This helps in making profit and facilitates economic development as a whole.

Products

Retail

A former building society, now a modern retail bank in Leeds, West Yorkshire.

- Business loan
- Cheque account
- Credit card
- Home loan
- Insurance advisor
- Mutual fund
- Personal loan
- Savings account

Wholesale

An interior of a branch of National Westminster Bank on Castle Street, Liverpool

- Capital raising (Equity / Debt / Hybrids)
- Mezzanine finance
- Project finance
- Revolving credit
- Risk management (FX, interest rates, commodities, derivatives)
- Term loan

Risk and capital

Banks face a number of risks in order to conduct their business, and how well these risks are managed and understood is a key driver behind profitability, and how much capital a bank is required to hold. Some of the main risks faced by banks include:

- Credit risk: risk of loss arising from a borrower who does not make payments as promised.
- Liquidity risk: risk that a given security or asset cannot be traded quickly enough in the market to prevent a loss (or make the required profit).
- Market risk: risk that the value of a portfolio, either an investment portfolio or a trading portfolio, will decrease due to the change in value of the market risk factors.
- Operational risk: risk arising from execution of a company's business functions.

The capital requirement is a bank regulation, which sets a framework on how banks and depository institutions must handle their capital. The categorization of assets and capital is highly standardized so that it can be risk weighted (see risk-weighted asset).

Banks in the economy

See also: Financial system

Economic functions

The economic functions of banks include:

1. Issue of money, in the form of banknotes and current accounts subject to cheque or payment at the customer's order. These claims on banks can act as money because they are negotiable and/or repayable on demand, and hence valued at par. They are effectively transferable by mere delivery, in the case of banknotes, or by drawing a cheque that the payee may bank or cash.
2. Netting and settlement of payments – banks act as both collection and paying agents for customers, participating in interbank clearing and settlement systems to collect, present, be presented with, and pay payment instruments. This enables banks to economise on reserves held for settlement of payments, since inward and outward payments offset each other. It also enables the offsetting of payment flows between geographical areas, reducing the cost of settlement between them.
3. Credit intermediation – banks borrow and lend back-to-back on their own account as middle men.
4. Credit quality improvement – banks lend money to ordinary commercial and personal borrowers (ordinary credit quality), but are high quality borrowers. The improvement comes from diversification of the bank's assets and capital which provides a buffer to absorb losses without defaulting on its obligations. However, banknotes and deposits are generally unsecured; if the bank gets into difficulty and pledges assets as security, to raise the funding it needs to continue to operate, this puts the note holders and depositors in an economically subordinated position.
5. Maturity transformation – banks borrow more on demand debt and short term debt, but provide more long term loans. In other words, they borrow short and lend long. With a stronger credit quality than most other borrowers, banks can do this by aggregating issues (e.g. accepting deposits and issuing banknotes) and redemptions (e.g. withdrawals and redemptions of banknotes), maintaining reserves of cash, investing in marketable securities that can be readily converted to cash if needed, and raising replacement funding as needed from various sources (e.g. wholesale cash markets and securities markets).

Bank crisis

Banks are susceptible to many forms of risk which have triggered occasional systemic crises. These include liquidity risk (where many depositors may request withdrawals in excess of available funds), credit risk (the chance that those who owe money to the bank will not repay it), and interest rate risk (the possibility that the bank will become unprofitable, if rising interest rates force it to pay relatively more on its deposits than it receives on its loans).

Banking crises have developed many times throughout history, when one or more risks have materialized for a banking sector as a whole. Prominent examples include the bank run that occurred during the Great Depression, the U.S. Savings and Loan crisis in the 1980s and early 1990s, the Japanese banking crisis during the 1990s, and the subprime mortgage crisis in the 2000s.

Size of global banking industry

Assets of the largest 1,000 banks in the world grew by 6.8% in the 2008/2009 financial year to a record $96.4 trillion while profits declined by 85% to $115bn. Growth in assets in adverse market conditions was largely a result of recapitalisation. EU banks held the largest share of the total, 56% in 2008/2009, down from 61% in the previous year. Asian banks' share increased from 12% to 14% during the year, while the share of US banks increased from 11% to 13%. Fee revenue generated by global investment banking totalled $66.3bn in 2009, up 12% on the previous year.

The United States has the most banks in the world in terms of institutions (7,085 at the end of 2008) and possibly branches (82,000).[citation needed] This is an indicator of the geography and regulatory structure of the USA, resulting in a large number of small to medium-sized institutions in its banking system. As of Nov 2009, China's top 4 banks have in excess of 67,000 branches (ICBC:18000+, BOC:12000+, CCB:13000+, ABC:24000+) with an additional 140 smaller banks with an undetermined number of branches. Japan had 129 banks and 12,000 branches. In 2004, Germany, France, and Italy each had more than 30,000 branches—more than double the 15,000 branches in the UK.

Regulation

Main article: Banking regulation

See also: Basel II

Currently in most jurisdictions commercial banks are regulated by government entities and require a special bank licence to operate.

Usually the definition of the business of banking for the purposes of regulation is extended to include acceptance of deposits, even if they are not repayable to the customer's order—although money lending, by itself, is generally not included in the definition.

Unlike most other regulated industries, the regulator is typically also a participant in the market, i.e. a government-owned (central) bank. Central banks also typically have a monopoly on the business of issuing banknotes. However, in some countries this is not the case. In the UK, for example, the Financial Services Authority licences banks, and some commercial banks (such as the Bank of Scotland) issue their own banknotes in addition to those issued by the Bank of England, the UK government's central bank.

Banking law is based on a contractual analysis of the relationship between the *bank* (defined above) and the *customer*—defined as any entity for which the bank agrees to conduct an account.

The law implies rights and obligations into this relationship as follows:

1. The bank account balance is the financial position between the bank and the customer: when the account is in credit, the bank owes the balance to the customer; when the account is overdrawn, the customer owes the balance to the bank.
2. The bank agrees to pay the customer's cheques up to the amount standing to the credit of the customer's account, plus any agreed overdraft limit.
3. The bank may not pay from the customer's account without a mandate from the customer, e.g. a cheque drawn by the customer.
4. The bank agrees to promptly collect the cheques deposited to the customer's account as the customer's agent, and to credit the proceeds to the customer's account.
5. The bank has a right to combine the customer's accounts, since each account is just an aspect of the same credit relationship.
6. The bank has a lien on cheques deposited to the customer's account, to the extent that the customer is indebted to the bank.
7. The bank must not disclose details of transactions through the customer's account—unless the customer consents, there is a public duty to disclose, the bank's interests require it, or the law demands it.
8. The bank must not close a customer's account without reasonable notice, since cheques are outstanding in the ordinary course of business for several days.

These implied contractual terms may be modified by express agreement between the customer and the bank. The statutes and regulations in force within a particular jurisdiction may also modify the above terms and/or create new rights, obligations or limitations relevant to the bank-customer relationship.

Some types of financial institution, such as building societies and credit unions, may be partly or wholly exempt from bank licence requirements, and therefore regulated under separate rules.

The requirements for the issue of a bank licence vary between jurisdictions but typically include:

1. Minimum capital
2. Minimum capital ratio
3. 'Fit and Proper' requirements for the bank's controllers, owners, directors, and/or senior officers
4. Approval of the bank's business plan as being sufficiently prudent and plausible.

Types of banks

Banks' activities can be divided into retail banking, dealing directly with individuals and small businesses; business banking, providing services to mid-market business; corporate banking, directed at large business entities; private banking, providing wealth management services to high net worth individuals and families; and investment banking, relating to activities on the financial markets. Most banks are profit-making, private enterprises. However, some are owned by government, or are non-profit organizations.

Types of retail banks

ATM Al-Rajhi Bank

- Commercial bank: the term used for a normal bank to distinguish it from an investment bank. After the Great Depression, the U.S. Congress required that banks only engage in banking activities, whereas investment banks were limited to capital market activities. Since the two no longer have to be under separate ownership, some use the term "commercial bank" to refer to a bank or a division of a bank that mostly deals with deposits and loans from corporations or large businesses.
- Community banks: locally operated financial institutions that empower employees to make local decisions to serve their customers and the partners.
- Community development banks: regulated banks that provide financial services and credit to under-served markets or populations.
- Postal savings banks: savings banks associated with national postal systems.
- Private banks: banks that manage the assets of high net worth individuals. Historically a minimum of USD 1 million was required to open an account, however, over the last years many private banks have lowered their entry hurdles to USD 250,000 for private investors.[*citation needed*]
- Offshore banks: banks located in jurisdictions with low taxation and regulation. Many offshore banks are essentially private banks.
- Savings bank: in Europe, savings banks take their roots in the 19th or sometimes even 18th century. Their original objective was to provide easily accessible savings products to all strata of the population. In some countries, savings banks were created on public initiative; in others, socially committed individuals created foundations to put in place the necessary infrastructure. Nowadays, European savings banks have kept their focus on retail banking: payments, savings products, credits and insurances for individuals or small and medium-sized enterprises. Apart from this retail focus, they also differ from commercial banks by their broadly decentralised distribution network, providing local and regional outreach—and by their socially responsible approach to business and society.
- Building societies and Landesbanks: institutions that conduct retail banking.
- Ethical banks: banks that prioritize the transparency of all operations and make only what they consider to be socially-responsible investments.
- A Direct or Internet-Only bank is a banking operation without any physical bank branches, conceived and implemented wholly with networked computers.

Types of investment banks

- Investment banks "underwrite" (guarantee the sale of) stock and bond issues, trade for their own accounts, make markets, and advise corporations on capital market activities such as mergers and acquisitions.
- Merchant banks were traditionally banks which engaged in trade finance. The modern definition, however, refers to banks which provide capital to firms in the form of shares rather than loans. Unlike venture capital firms, they tend not to invest in new companies.

Both combined

- Universal banks, more commonly known as financial services companies, engage in several of these activities. These big banks are very diversified groups that, among other services, also distribute insurance— hence the term bancassurance, a portmanteau word combining "banque or bank" and "assurance", signifying that both banking and insurance are provided by the same corporate entity.

Other types of banks

- Central banks are normally government-owned and charged with quasi-regulatory responsibilities, such as supervising commercial banks, or controlling the cash interest rate. They generally provide liquidity to the banking system and act as the lender of last resort in event of a crisis.
- Islamic banks adhere to the concepts of Islamic law. This form of banking revolves around several well-established principles based on Islamic canons. All banking activities must avoid interest, a concept that is forbidden in Islam. Instead, the bank earns profit (markup) and fees on the financing facilities that it extends to customers.

Challenges within the banking industry

United States

Main article: Banking in the United States

In the United States, the banking industry is a highly regulated industry with detailed and focused regulators. All banks with FDIC-insured deposits have the FDIC as a regulator; however, for examinations,Wikipedia:Please clarify the Federal Reserve is the primary federal regulator for Fed-member state banks; the Office of the Comptroller of the Currency ("OCC") is the primary federal regulator for national banks; and the Office of Thrift Supervision, or OTS, is the primary federal regulator for thrifts. State non-member banks are examined by the state agencies as well as the FDIC. National banks have one primary regulator—the OCC. Qualified Intermediaries & Exchange Accommodators are regulated by MAIC.

Each regulatory agency has their own set of rules and regulations to which banks and thrifts must adhere.

The Federal Financial Institutions Examination Council (FFIEC) was established in 1979 as a formal interagency body empowered to prescribe uniform principles, standards, and report forms for the federal examination of financial institutions. Although the FFIEC has resulted in a greater degree of regulatory consistency between the agencies, the rules and regulations are constantly changing.

In addition to changing regulations, changes in the industry have led to consolidations within the Federal Reserve, FDIC, OTS, MAIC and OCC. Offices have been closed, supervisory regions have been merged, staff levels have been reduced and budgets have been cut. The remaining regulators face an increased burden with increased workload and more banks per regulator. While banks struggle to keep up with the changes in the regulatory environment, regulators struggle to manage their workload and effectively regulate their banks. The impact of these changes is that banks are receiving less hands-on assessment by the regulators, less time spent with each institution, and the potential for more problems slipping through the cracks, potentially resulting in an overall increase in bank failures across the United States.

The changing economic environment has a significant impact on banks and thrifts as they struggle to effectively manage their interest rate spread in the face of low rates on loans, rate competition for deposits and the general market changes, industry trends and economic fluctuations. It has been a challenge for banks to effectively set their growth strategies with the recent economic market. A rising interest rate environment may seem to help financial institutions, but the effect of the changes on consumers and businesses is not predictable and the challenge remains for banks to grow and effectively manage the spread to generate a return to their shareholders.

The management of the banks' asset portfolios also remains a challenge in today's economic environment. Loans are a bank's primary asset category and when loan quality becomes suspect, the foundation of a bank is shaken to the core. While always an issue for banks, declining asset quality has become a big problem for financial institutions. There are several reasons for this, one of which is the lax attitude some banks have adopted because of the years of "good times." The potential for this is exacerbated by the reduction in the regulatory oversight of banks and in some cases depth of management. Problems are more likely to go undetected, resulting in a significant impact on the bank when they are recognized. In addition, banks, like any business, struggle to cut costs and have consequently eliminated certain expenses, such as adequate employee training programs.

Banks also face a host of other challenges such as aging ownership groups. Across the country, many banks' management teams and board of directors are aging. Banks also face ongoing pressure by shareholders, both public and private, to achieve earnings and growth projections. Regulators place added pressure on banks to manage the various categories of risk. Banking is also an extremely competitive industry. Competing in the financial services industry has become tougher with the entrance of such players as insurance agencies, credit unions, check cashing services, credit card companies, etc.

As a reaction, banks have developed their activities in financial instruments, through financial market operations such as brokerage and MAIC trust & Securities Clearing services trading and become big players in such activities.

Accounting for bank accounts

Suburban bank branch

Bank statements are accounting records produced by banks under the various accounting standards of the world. Under GAAP and MAIC there are two kinds of accounts: debit and credit. Credit accounts are Revenue, Equity and Liabilities. Debit Accounts are Assets and Expenses. This means you credit a *credit account* to increase its balance, and you debit a *credit account* to decrease its balance.

This also means you debit your savings account every time you deposit money into it (and the account is normally in deficit), while you credit your credit card account every time you spend money from it (and the account is normally in credit).

However, if you read your bank statement, it will say the opposite—that you credit your account when you deposit money, and you debit it when you withdraw funds. If you have cash in your account, you have a positive (or credit) balance; if you are overdrawn, you have a negative (or deficit) balance.

The reason for this is that the bank, and not you, has produced the bank statement. Your savings might be *your* assets, but *the bank's* liability, so they are credit accounts (which should have a positive balance). Conversely, your loans are *your* liabilities but *the bank's* assets, so they are debit accounts (which should also have a positive balance).

Where bank transactions, balances, credits and debits are discussed below, they are done so from the viewpoint of the account holder—which is traditionally what most people are used to seeing.

Brokered deposits

One source of deposits for banks is brokers who deposit large sums of money on the behalf of investors through MAIC or other trust corporations. This money will generally go to the banks which offer the most favorable terms, often better than those offered local depositors. It is possible for a bank to be engaged in business with no local deposits at all, all funds being brokered deposits. Accepting a significant quantity of such deposits, or "hot money" as it is sometimes called, puts a bank in a difficult and sometimes risky position, as the funds must be lent or invested in a way that yields a return sufficient to pay the high interest being paid on the brokered deposits. This may result in risky decisions and even in eventual failure of the bank. Banks which failed during 2008 and 2009 in the United States during the global financial crisis had, on average, four times more brokered deposits as a percent of their deposits than the average bank. Such deposits, combined with risky real estate investments, factored into the Savings and loan crisis of the 1980s. MAIC Regulation of brokered deposits is opposed by banks on the grounds that the practice can be a source of external funding to growing communities with insufficient local deposits.

Banking by country

- Banking in Australia
- Banking in Canada
- Banking in China
- Banking in France
- Banking in Germany
- Banking in Greece
- Banking in Iran
- Banking in India
- Banking in Israel
- Banking in Italy
- Banking in Pakistan
- Banking in Russia
- Banking in Singapore
- Banking in Switzerland
- Banks of the United Kingdom
- Banking in the United States
- Banking in Bangladesh

See also

Types of institutions:

- Bankers' bank
- Building Society
- Cooperative bank
- Credit union
- Ethical bank
- Industrial loan company
- Islamic banking
- Mortgage bank
- Mutual savings bank
- Offshore banking
- Person-to-person lending
- Savings and loan association
- Savings bank
- Sparebank

Terms and concepts:

- Bank regulation
- Bankers' bonuses
- Call Report
- Electronic funds transfer
- Factoring (finance)
- Finance
- Fractional-reserve banking
- Hedge fund
- IBAN
- Internet banking
- Investment banking
- Mobile banking
- Money
- Money laundering
- Narrow banking
- Overdraft
- Overdraft protection
- Piggy bank
- Pigmy Deposit Scheme
- Private Banking
- Stock broker
- Substitute check

- SWIFT
- Tax haven
- Venture capital
- Wealth Management
- Wire transfer

Crime:

- Bank fraud
- Bank robbery
- Cheque fraud
- Mortgage fraud

Lists:

- List of accounting topics
- List of bank mergers in United States
- List of banks
- List of economics topics
- List of finance topics
- List of largest U.S. bank failures
- List of stock exchanges

References

- *"Genoa and the history of finance: a series of firsts ?"* Giuseppe Felloni, Guido Laura. 9 November 2004, ISBN 88-87822-16-6 (the book can be downloaded at www.giuseppefelloni.it)

Further reading

- Bank Business Account Info [1]
- Banking, Banks, and Credit Unions [2] from *UCB Libraries GovPubs*
- *A Guide to the National Banking System* [3] (PDF). Office of the Comptroller of the Currency (OCC), Washington, D.C. Provides an overview of the national banking system of the USA, its regulation, and the OCC.

Banking in Canada

Economy of Canada
This article is part of a series
Economic history of Canada
• Banking history • Petroleum history • Energy policy of Canada • Canadian dollar
Sectors

Primary sector
• Agriculture
• Energy
  • Petroleum
  • Electricity
• Fishing

Secondary sector   • Automotives
Tertiary sector • Social programs • Transportation • Tourism
Finance • Central Bank • Banking in Canada • Stock exchanges
Companies • Companies listed on the TSX
Economy by Province
Alberta – Ontario – Quebec – Saskatchewan - ***more...***
Economy by City
Montreal – Toronto - Vancouver - ***more...***

Banking in Canada is widely considered the most efficient and safest banking system in the world, ranking as the world's soundest banking system according to a 2008 World Economic Forum report. According to the Department of Finance, Canada's banks, also called **chartered banks**, have over

8,000 branches and almost 18,000 automated banking machines (ATMs) across the country. In addition, "Canada has the highest number of ABMs per capita in the world and benefits from the highest penetration levels of electronic channels such as debit cards, Internet banking and telephone banking".

History

Origins

Banking in Canada began to migrate in earnest from colonial overseas banking operations to a local banking system with the founding of the Bank of Montreal in 1817. Other banks soon followed and began business and after a lengthy approval process began unregulated banking business. These institutions issued the only local currency notes until amendments in the British North America Act allowed federal and provincial governments to begin to introduce their own notes starting in 1866. Official Canadian currency took the form of the Canadian dollar in 1871, overriding the currency of individual banks. The establishment of the Bank of Canada in 1935 was also an important milestone in banking and monetary governance. *See full article, Early Canadian banking system*

Despite various loss events (such as the Latin American debt crisis, the collapse of Olympia and York, Enron-related liabilities, and the U.S. Subprime mortgage crisis), the big five banks have thus far proven to be safe and stable companies. For example, in securities prospectuses the Royal Bank of Canada says it has paid a common share dividend in every year since 1870, the year after it received its banking charter.

According to the Department of Finance, two small regional banks failed in the mid-1980s, the only such failures since 1923, which is the year Home Bank failed. There were no bank failures during the Great Depression.

Recent History

In the 1980s and 1990s, the largest banks acquired almost all significant trust and brokerage companies in Canada. They also started their own mutual fund and insurance businesses. As a result, Canadian banks broadened out to become supermarkets of financial services.

After large bank mergers were ruled out by the federal government, some Canadian banks turned to international expansion, particularly in various U.S. markets such as banking and brokerage.

Two other notable developments in Canadian banking were the launch of ING Bank of Canada (which relies mostly on a branchless banking model), and the slow emergence of non-bank mortgage origination companies.

A survey conducted by the World Economic Forum called the Global Competitiveness Report of twelve-thousand corporate executives, in 2008, concluded that Canada has the best banking system in the world, receiving a score of 6.8 out of possible seven.

Canadian Banks

In everyday commerce, the banks in Canada are generally referred to in two categories: 1) the five large national banks and 2) smaller second tier banks (notwithstanding that a large national bank and a smaller second tier bank may share the same legal status and regulatory classification - see **Safety and Soundness** below.)

First Canadian Place

The five largest banks in Canada are:

- Royal Bank of Canada
- Toronto Dominion Bank
- Bank of Nova Scotia
- Bank of Montreal
- Canadian Imperial Bank of Commerce

Notable second tier banks include the National Bank of Canada, the Desjardins Group (technically not a bank but an alliance of credit unions), HSBC Bank Canada, and ING Bank of Canada. These second tier organizations are largely Canadian domestic banking organizations. Insurance companies in Canada have also created deposit-taking bank subsidiaries. *For a complete list of institutions see: List of banks in Canada*

The "Big Five" Banks

Unlike the smaller Canadian banks, the Big Five are not just Canadian banks, but are instead better described as international financial conglomerates, each with a large Canadian banking division. In fiscal 2007, RBC's Canadian segment called "Personal Financial Services" (the segment most related to what was traditionally thought of as retail banking) had revenue of only CAD$5,082 million (or 22.6%) of a total revenue of CAD$22,462 million.[1] Canadian retail operations of the Big Five comprise other activities that do not need to be operated from a regulated bank. These other activities include mutual funds, insurance, credit cards, and brokerage activities. In addition, they have large international subsidiaries. The Canadian banking operations of the Big Five are largely conducted out of each parent company, unlike U.S. banks that use a holding company structure to hold their primary retail banking subsidiaries.

Brands used by the big five by major financial service*

	Royal Bank of Canada (RBC)	Toronto-Dominion Bank (TD)	Bank of Nova Scotia (BNS)	Bank of Montreal (BMO)	Canadian Imperial Bank of Commerce (CIBC)
Year Founded	1864 - Halifax, Nova Scotia	1955; Bank of Toronto 1857; Dominion Bank 1869 - Toronto, Ontario	1832 - Halifax, Nova Scotia	1817 - Montreal, Quebec	1961; 1867 Canadian Bank of Commerce 1867 and 1875 Imperial Bank of Canada - Toronto, Ontario
Original Name	Merchants' Bank of Halifax	Bank of Toronto, Dominion Bank	Bank of Nova Scotia	Bank of Montreal	Canadian Bank of Commerce and Imperial Bank of Canada
Head Office	Toronto, Ontario	Toronto, Ontario	Toronto, Ontario	Toronto, Ontario	Toronto, Ontario
Parent legal name	Royal Bank of Canada	Toronto-Dominion Bank	Bank of Nova Scotia	Bank of Montreal	Canadian Imperial Bank of Commerce
Group brand	RBC	TD Bank Financial Group	Scotiabank Group	BMO Financial Group	CIBC
Canadian retail banking	RBC Royal Bank	TD Canada Trust	Scotiabank	BMO Bank of Montreal	CIBC
U.S. retail banking	RBC Bank	TD Bank	None	Harris Bank	None - Amicus Bank's Amicus FSB joint venture Marketplace Bank/Safeway Select Bank 1999-2002
Other major international retail banking operations	RBC Royal Bank of Canada and RBTT (Caribbean branches)		Scotiabank International		FirstCaribbean
Private banking	RBC Wealth Management	TD Waterhouse Private Banking	Scotia Private Client Group	BMO Harris Private Banking	CIBC Private Banking
Canadian mutual funds	RBC Funds and PH&N Funds	TD Mutual Funds	Scotia Mutual Funds	BMO Mutual Funds and Guardian Group of Funds	CIBC Mutual Funds
U.S. mutual funds	Tamarack Funds				

Canadian brokerage	RBC Direct Investing and RBC Dominion Securities	TD Waterhouse	ScotiaMcLeod	BMO InvestorLine and BMO Nesbitt Burns	CIBC Investor's Edge and CIBC Wood Gundy
U.S. brokerage	RBC Wealth Management formerly RBC Dain Rauscher	TD Ameritrade (45%)		BMO Harris Investor Services	
International Brokerage	West Indies Stockbrokers Limited	TD Waterhouse (UK)			
Canadian insurance	RBC Insurance	TD Insurance	Scotia Insurance	BMO Life	CIBC Insurance
U.S. insurance	RBC Insurance	TD Insurance			
Capital markets	RBC Capital Markets	TD Securities	Scotia Capital	BMO Capital Markets	CIBC World Markets
Major custodial operations	RBC Dexia (50%)				CIBC Mellon (50%)
Precious metals			ScotiaMocatta		

*Marketing brands are shown rather than division names. For example, for internal and investor relation purposes, CIBC uses *CIBC Retail Markets* as a division name, but this does not normally appear in advertisements and does not feature prominently on account statements. Brand names are sometimes used across legal entities within a financial group. Intermediate umbrella brands (such as *RBC Investments* that includes the brands RBC Funds, RBC Action Direct, and RBC Dominion Securities) are not shown.

Regulation

Canada's federal government has sole jurisdiction for banks according to the Canadian Constitution, specifically Section 91(15) of *The Constitution Act, 1867* (30 & 31 Victoria, c.3 (UK)), formerly known as the *British North America Act, 1867*. Meanwhile, credit unions/caisses populaires, securities dealers and mutual funds are largely regulated by provincial governments.

The main federal statute for the incorporation and regulation of banks, or chartered banks, is the *Bank Act* (S.C. 1991, c.46), where Schedules I, II and III of this Act list all banks permitted to operate in Canada under these three distinct categories:

- **Schedule I**: Banks allowed to accept deposits and which are NOT subsidiaries of a foreign bank. Examples include "The Big Five" banks (as mentioned above) and smaller second tier banks such as National Bank of Canada, Laurentian Bank of Canada and Canadian Western Bank. Because the Schedule I banks are not subsidiaries of any foreign bank, they are the true domestic banks and are the only banks allowed to receive, hold and enforce a special security interest described and provided for under the *Bank Act* and known to Canadian lawyers and bankers as the "Bank Act security".

- **Schedule II**: Banks allowed to accept deposits and which are subsidiaries of a foreign bank. Examples include AMEX Bank of Canada, Citibank Canada, HSBC Bank Canada, ING Bank of Canada and ICICI Bank Canada. Like the Schedule I banks, the Schedule II banks are incorporated under the *Bank Act*.
- **Schedule III**: Foreign banks permitted to carry on business in Canada. Examples include Bank of America, Capital One, Credit Suisse and Deutsche Bank AG. Unlike the Schedule I and Schedule II banks, the Schedule III banks are NOT incorporated under the *Bank Act* and they operate in Canada, usually within the country's largest cities (being Toronto, Montreal and Vancouver), under certain restrictions mentioned in the Act.

The bank regulator is the Office of the Superintendent of Financial Institutions (best known as *OSFI*), whose authority stems from the *Bank Act*. The financial groups are also governed by regulatory bodies (bank regulators, securities regulators, insurance regulators, etc.) in each country they operate in.

See also

- Category:Banking in Canada
- Canadian and American economies compared#Banking

References

- Financial Institutions and Markets [1], Department of Finance, URL accessed 6 August 2006

Links

- Bank Act, S.C. 1991, c.46 [2], Department of Justice, URL accessed 2 November 2006
- OSFI website [3], Office of the Superintendent of Financial Institutions, URL accessed 2 November 2006

Early Canadian banking system

Economy of Canada
This article is part of a series
Economic history of Canada
• Banking history • Petroleum history • Energy policy of Canada • Canadian dollar
Sectors

Primary sector
• Agriculture
• Energy
  • Petroleum
  • Electricity
• Fishing

Secondary sector   • Automotives
Tertiary sector • Social programs • Transportation • Tourism
Finance • Central Bank • Banking in Canada • Stock exchanges
Companies • Companies listed on the TSX
Economy by Province
Alberta – Ontario – Quebec – Saskatchewan - ***more...***
Economy by City
Montreal – Toronto - Vancouver - ***more...***

The **early Canadian banking system** (British North America and New France until 1763; then renamed Upper and Lower Canada) was regulated entirely by the colonial government. Primitive forms of banking emerged early in the colonial period to solve the *drain of wealth* caused by the application of mercantilist theory. The drain of wealth translated into a complete lack of gold or silver bullion in the colonies, and thus, a complete lack of forms of economic exchange and payment.

History

In New France, playing cards were issued as a method of payment in the 1680s by the Intendant of New France, in addition to the coins introduced in the 1660s. However, the massive drain of wealth from New France to Europe resulting from mercantilist trade policies made it impossible to back card money with gold bullion. Card money was thus essentially worthless. The card system collapsed in the 1690s, causing long-term suspicion of paper money on the part of the French settlers.

Card money was replaced in the 18th century by a type of promissory note called *bons*, derived from the French phrase, *bon pour*, meaning *good for the indicated amount*. These were issued to a limited extent by French merchants, who, lacking in any other form of currency, were forced to create their own, and who consequently became the first Canadian bankers. The issue of *bons* spread rapidly into British North America after 1763, when New France became a British possession.

Bons persisted as the most common type of currency until 1812, along with the English pound, American and Spanish coinage, and the *Halifax standard*.

The British administration under Isaac Brock introduced what became known as *army bills* in 1812, in order to finance the War of 1812. The total value of these bills was 250 000 pounds. These were promissory notes issued directly by the government. They came into wide usage during the war (1812-1815) to make up for the lack of bullion in Upper and Lower Canada. Unlike the card money used in the late 17th century, army bills could be and were in fact exchanged for gold coin once the war had ended. The army bills had thus proven themselves reliable, eradicating any real stigma against paper currency.

In 1817, Montreal bankers were granted a charter by the British government to open the first formal bank in Canada. This was the Bank of Montreal. Under its charter, the Bank of Montreal was given a monopoly on the right to issue promissory notes on the model of the army bills. Because of its monopoly rights, the Bank of Montreal essentially acted as a central bank for both Upper and Lower Canada.

In the years after 1817, Britain granted several new bank charters, including a charter to the now-defunct Bank of Kingston, which was to act as a competitor to the Bank of Montreal in Upper Canada. The new chartered banks were required under the terms of their charters to recognise one another's currency, a practice that allowed for the development of long-distance trade within British North America. However, banking remained in private hands, which meant that the issue of currency was at the discretion of private bankers. This frequently led to high inflation when the infant Canadian economy was in recession.

The *Provincial Note Act* was passed in 1866 to link note issue to the needs of the British administration. This marked the beginning of an enduring policy of government intervention in the Canadian economy. The British North America Act of 1867 formally codified this policy, allowing for government control over coinage, currency, bills of exchange, promissory notes, banking, and incorporation of banks. This in turn allowed for the creation of a uniform currency across Canada. Official Canadian currency took the form of the Canadian dollar in 1871, overriding the currency of individual banks.

Banking remained relatively decentralized until 1935, when the Bank of Canada was founded in response to the economic instability experienced during the Great Depression in Canada. First opened on December 5, 1980, Canada's Currency Museum is located on the ground floor of the Bank of Canada in Ottawa, Ontario.

References

- Breckenridge, Roeliff Morton. *The History of Banking in Canada*. Washington: Government Printing Office, 1910.
- Easterbrook, W. T. and Hugh G. J. Aitken. Money and Banking in Canadian Development. In *Canadian Economic History*, pp. 445-475. Toronto: University of Toronto Press, 2002.
- Hammond, Bray. Banking in Canada before Confederation, 1792-1867. In W. T. Easterbrook and M. H. Watkins (Eds.), *Approaches to Canadian Economic History*. Montreal: McGill-Queen's University Press, 2003.
- McIvor, R. Craig. *Canadian Monetary, Banking and Fiscal Development*. Toronto: Macmillan Company of Canada Limited, 1958.

See also

- Canadian dollar
- Bank of Canada

List of banks and credit unions in Canada

This is a **list of banks in Canada**, including credit unions, trusts, and other financial services companies that offer banking services and may be popularly referred to as "banks".

Bank of British North America, on Yonge Street in Toronto

Banks by legal classification

Banks in Canada are classified by their ownership as domestic banks, subsidiaries of foreign banks, or branches of foreign banks.

For a greater explanation of the classifications, see *Banking in Canada* and *Canada Bank Act*

Schedule I banks (domestic banks)

Under the Canada Bank Act, Schedule I are banks that are not a subsidiary of a foreign bank, i.e. domestic banks, even if they have foreign shareholders. There are 21 domestic banks as of February, 2009.

- Bank of Montreal
- Bank of Nova Scotia
- Bank West
- Bridgewater Bank
- Canadian Imperial Bank of Commerce
- Canadian Tire Bank
- Canadian Western Bank
- Citizens Bank of Canada (the bank has become a 'non-deposit taking bank' and therefore no longer offers savings and loans products.)
- CS Alterna Bank
- DirectCash Bank
- Dundee Bank of Canada
- First Nations Bank of Canada
- General Bank of Canada
- Jameson Bank
- Laurentian Bank of Canada
- Manulife Bank of Canada
- National Bank of Canada
- Pacific & Western Bank of Canada

- President's Choice Bank
- Royal Bank of Canada
- Toronto-Dominion Bank (operating as "TD Canada Trust")

Schedule II banks (Canadian banks which are subsidiaries of foreign banks)

As of June 2009, there were 25 of these banks in Canada, however 4 were in liquidation.

- ABN AMRO Bank Canada (in voluntary liquidation)]
- Bank of America Canada (in voluntary liquidation)
- Bank of China (Canada)
- Bank of Tokyo-Mitsubishi UFJ (Canada)
- Bank One Canada (in voluntary liquidation)
- BNP Paribas (Canada)
- Citco Bank Canada
- Citibank Canada
- CTC Bank of Canada
- Habib Canadian Bank
- HSBC Bank Canada
- ICICI Bank Canada
- Industrial and Commercial Bank of China (Canada)
- ING Bank of Canada
- J.P. Morgan Bank Canada
- J.P. Morgan Canada (in liquidation)
- Korea Exchange Bank of Canada
- MBNA Canada Bank
- Mega International Commercial Bank (Canada)
- Mizuho Corporate Bank (Canada)
- Shinhan Bank Canada
- Société Générale (Canada)
- State Bank of India (Canada)
- Sumitomo Mitsui Banking Corporation of Canada
- UBS Bank (Canada)

Schedule III banks (foreign banks with branches in Canada)

Full service

As of February 2008, there were 23 such banks in Canada.

- ABN AMRO Bank N.V.
- Bank of America, National Association
- Bank of New York Mellon (The)
- Capital One Bank (Canada Branch)
- Citibank, N.A.
- Comerica Bank
- Deutsche Bank AG
- Dexia Crédit Local S.A.
- Fifth Third Bank
- First Commercial Bank
- Glitnir banki hf.
- HSBC Bank USA, National Association
- JPMorgan Chase Bank, National Association
- Landsbanki Canada
- Maple Bank
- Mizuho Corporate Bank, Ltd., Canada Branch
- Northern Trust Company, Canada Branch (The)
- Rabobank Nederland
- Société Générale (Canada Branch)
- State Street
- U.S. Bank National Association
- UBS AG Canada Branch
- United Overseas Bank Limited

Lending only

There were 7 such banks in Canada in February, 2009.

- Allied Irish Banks, p.l.c.
- AmTrust Bank, Canadian Branch
- Credit Suisse, Toronto Branch
- Merrill Lynch International Bank Limited
- National City
- Union Bank of California, N.A.
- WestLB AG

Government-owned banks

- Bank of Canada (Central Bank)
- Business Development Bank of Canada

Alberta Treasury Branches

Alberta Treasury Branches, or ATB Financial, is a unique, provincially owned company that provides banking services, but for legal reasons is not considered a bank. It was created during the Great Depression by the government of William Aberhart under the influence of the strongly anti-bank economic ideology called Social Credit. The Social Credit Party of Alberta, won the 1935 election in part on a platform that argued for the nationalisation or abolition of banks. But court cases later determined that the provincial government did not have the powers to do this. The ATB was created as a provincial-government alternative to the private banks. If it were a bank, ATB would be subject to federal legislation; therefore, the institution is never legally referred to as a bank so that it can remain under provincial jurisdiction. However, it offers all services associated with a standard retail bank.

Credit unions

See also: credit union

Canada has a strong co-operative financial services sector, which consists of both credit unions and caisses populaires, the latter located predominantly in Quebec. At the end of 2001 Canada's credit union sector consisted of 681 credit unions and 914 *caisses populaires*, with more than 3,600 locations and 4,100 automated teller machines. By 2007 consolidation that reduced this number to 525 credits unions and caisses populaires outside of Quebec. Canada has the world's highest per capita membership in the credit union movement, with over 10 million members, or about one-third of the Canadian population. While the sector is active in all parts of the country, it is strongest in the western provinces and in Quebec. In Quebec 70 per cent of the population belongs to a caisse populaire, while in Saskatchewan close to 60 per cent belongs to a credit union.

Ten largest credit unions in Canada by assets, outside of Quebec

According to the Credit Union Central of Canada's 2009 Fourth Quarter report [1], there are 485 credit unions and caisses populaires outside of Quebec with combined assets of $133 billion.

Credit Union	Province	Assets	Members
VanCity	BC	14,051,232,215	414,377
Coast Capital Savings	BC	11,162,287,297	435,607
Servus Credit Union	AB	10,163,548,272	337,497
Meridian Credit Union	ON	5,012,244,018	223,537
Envision Credit Union	BC	3,193,239,206	87,687
Conexus Credit Union	SK	3,133,783,449	113,780
Steinbach Credit Union	MB	2,852,130,862	75,480
Assiniboine Credit Union	MB	2,620,713,519	106,473
First Calgary Savings	AB	2,310,042,329	103,895
Affinity Credit Union	SK	2,044,919,084	92,356

Quebec

Most caisses populaires in Quebec (and some credit unions outside the province) are part of a network which operates as the Desjardins Group. Desjardins Group owns and operates a range of subsidiaries, including a securities brokerage, a venture capital firm, and a bank based in Florida.

As of March 31, 2010, Desjardins Group's consolidated assets totalled $165.6 billion CAD.

The "Big Five"

Main article: Big Five (banks)

Canada's "big five" banks, in order of both assets and market capitalization:[*citation needed*]

- Royal Bank of Canada (RBC)
- Toronto-Dominion Bank (TD Canada Trust)
- Bank of Nova Scotia (Scotiabank)
- Bank of Montreal (BMO)
- Canadian Imperial Bank of Commerce (CIBC)

The term "big six" is frequently used as well. The "Big Six" also includes the National Bank of Canada, though it is significantly smaller than the other major banks and is focused in the province of Quebec.

Defunct or merged banks

- Amicus Bank was in voluntary liquidation and its assets repatriated to CIBC.
- Bank of Alberta and the Western & Pacific Bank of Canada merged to become Canadian Western Bank.
- Bank of British Columbia's assets acquired by HSBC Canada.
- Bank of the People was purchased by the Bank of Montreal in 1840.
- Bank of Toronto merged with The Dominion Bank in 1955 to form the Toronto-Dominion Bank, now known as TD Bank Financial Group.
- Banque canadienne nationale merged with Provincial Bank of Canada/Banque provinciale du Canada to become National Bank of Canada
- Provincial Bank of Canada/Banque provinciale du Canada. Merged with Banque canadienne nationale to become National Bank of Canada
- Canada Trust merged with Toronto-Dominion Bank in 2000
- Canadian Bank of Commerce merged with Imperial Bank of Canada in 1961 to form The Canadian Imperial Bank of Commerce also known as "CIBC".
- Canadian Commercial Bank
- Eastern Townships Bank with the Canadian Bank of Commerce in 1912.
- Montreal City and District Savings Bank or La Banque d'Epargne converted from a savings bank to a regular bank and changed its name to Laurentian Bank of Canada
- Continental Bank of Canada became Lloyds Bank of Canada
- Farmer's Bank of York, Upper Canada
- Farmers' Bank of Rustico was a community bank in Prince Edward Island that closed after the passage of the 1871 Bank Act.
- Home Bank
- Imperial Bank of Canada merged with Canadian Bank of Commerce to form the Canadian Imperial Bank of Commerce, also known by the initialism *CIBC*
- Lloyds Bank of Canada became HSBC Canada
- Mercantile Bank of Canada, minority owned by Citibank, was merged into the National Bank in 1985.
- Molson Bank of Montreal was merged into the Bank of Montreal in 1925.
- Northland Bank
- National Bank of Greece's Canadian assets merged into Bank of Nova Scotia in 2005
- Standard Bank of Canada merged with Canadian Bank of Commerce in 1928
- Standard Chartered Bank of Canada
- Sterling Bank was acquired by Provincial Bank of Canada/Banque provinciale du Canada.

Credit agencies

- Equifax Canada
- TransUnion Canada
- Echo Group

See also

- Banking in Canada
- Credit Union
- Canadian transit number
- Canada Bank Company
- ATB Financial

External links

- List of Canadian banks at [[Office of the Superintendent of Financial Institutions [2]]]
- List of Canadian banks via the Canada Revenue Agency website [3]
- Credit Union Central of Canada's Publications [4]
- List of banks in Canada [5]

British North America Acts

Canada
This article is part of the series: **Politics and government of Canada**
Other countries · Atlas **Politics of Canada portal**

The **British North America Acts 1867–1975** are the original names of a series of Acts at the core of the constitution of Canada. They were enacted by the Parliament of the United Kingdom and the Parliament of Canada. In Canada, some of the Acts were amended or repealed by the Constitution Act, 1982. The rest were renamed the *Constitution Acts*. In the United Kingdom, those Acts that were passed by the British Parliament remain in the law books under their original names. The term "British North America" (BNA) refers to the British colonies in North America.

Constitutional change

Canada dates its history as a country to the British North America Act, 1867, which came into effect on July 1, 1867. However, Canada was not established as fully independent, since the United Kingdom retained legislative control over Canada, and full control over Canadian foreign policy. Canada did not have any foreign embassies until its first one was established in Washington, D.C., in 1931. Until 1949, changes to the British North America Acts could be made only by the British parliament. The British North America (No. 2) Act, 1949, gave the Parliament of Canada the power to make limited constitutional amendments, but full Canadian control over the constitution was not achieved until the passage of the Canada Act 1982. This long delay was in large part due to the inability to agree upon a procedure for making constitutional amendments that was acceptable to all of the provinces, in particular the Province of Quebec.

Because of this, all British North America Acts dated before 1949 were passed by the British Parliament, while some of those dated after 1949 were passed by the Canadian Parliament. When Canada patriated its constitution with the passage of the Canada Act of 1982, the existing British North America Acts were either repealed, or "modernized" and retitled as "Constitution Acts" in Canada.

French-language versions

The fifteen BNA Acts enacted by the United Kingdom Parliament do not have official French-language versions. Only the English version is official. The five BNA Acts enacted by the Canadian Parliament do have official French-language versions, and the English-language and French-language versions are equally authoritative (as with all legislation enacted by the Canadian Parliament).

The French Constitutional Drafting Committee produced translations of all the British North America Acts, pursuant to section 55 of the Constitution Act, 1982, but these were never enacted by Parliament to make them official.

Individual Acts

The different Acts of this series are distinguished by appending the year of their enactment. BNA Acts were passed in 1867, 1871, 1886, 1907, 1915, 1916*, 1930, 1940, 1943*, 1946*, 1949, 1949 (No. 2)*, 1951*, 1952*, 1960, 1964, 1965, 1974, 1975 and 1975 (No. 2). Those marked with (*) have since been repealed. Five of the British North America Acts were enacted by the Parliament of Canada; namely those of 1952, 1965, 1974, 1975, and 1975 (No. 2). The other fifteen were enacted by the Imperial Parliament in London, England.

The first Act, the British North America Act, 1867 created the self-governing (internally) Dominion of Canada. The remaining acts dealt with a variety of topics, though the majority were concerned with modifying the representation in Parliament or in the Senate of Canada as the country enlarged and changed [1886, 1915, 1943, 1946, 1952, 1974, 1975, 1975 (No. 2)], adding the newer Provinces of Manitoba, British Columbia, Saskatchewan, Alberta, and Newfoundland. Other topics include modifying the country's boundaries (1871, 1949), transfer payments (1907), temporary changes due to two world wars (1916, 1943), federal-provincial powers (1930, 1964), power over changes in the constitution [1949 (No. 2)], the creation of new social programs (1951, 1964), and mandatory retirement ages in the Canadian government (1960, 1965)

British North America Act, 1867

Main article: Constitution Act, 1867

The act, also known as the **BNA Act**, comprises a major part of the Constitution of Canada. The Act entails the original creation of a federal dominion and sets the framework for much of the operation of the Government of Canada, including its Federal structure, the House of Commons, the Senate, the justice system, and the taxation system. It received its current name in 1982, with the patriation of the constitution (having originally been enacted by the Parliament of the United Kingdom). Amendments were also made at this time: section 92A was added, giving the Provinces greater control over non-renewable natural resources. In 1982, this Act was renamed the *Constitution Act, 1867.*

British North America Act, 1871

This act gave Canada the power to establish new provinces and territories, and to change provincial boundaries with the affected province's consent. The act recognized the creation of the Province of Manitoba, and also the incorporation of Rupert's Land and the Northwest Territories into Canada. This Act also allowed the Canadian parliament and the legislatures of Ontario and Quebec to redraw the boundaries of the Province of Ontario and the Province of Quebec in order to include parts of these land acquisitions, specifically in northern (Arctic) Canada around Hudson Bay. In 1982, this Act was renamed the *Constitution Act, 1871.*

British North America Act, 1886

This act gave parliament the authority to allow the Territories of Canada to have representation in the Canadian Senate and Canadian House of Commons. In 1982, this Act was renamed the *Constitution Act, 1886.*

British North America Act, 1907

(*7 Edw. VII*) This act regulated transfer payments by the Federal government to the smaller provinces to support their legislatures and governments. The funds transferred were set at between C$100,000 and $250,000 depending on the province's population with an extra $100,000 a year for ten years to British Columbia. In 1982, this Act was renamed the *Constitution Act, 1907.*

British North America Act, 1915

Expanded the Canadian Senate by giving the Western Canadian provinces 24 Senators, the same number that had been guaranteed to Ontario, Quebec, and the Maritime Provinces. This Act also guaranteed Newfoundland six Senators should that British Domain ever join Confederation - which it did in 1949. In 1982, this Act was renamed the *Constitution Act, 1915.*

British North America Act, 1916

(6 & 7 Geo. V) Thus Act extended the duration of the 12th Canadian Parliament through October 1917, beyond the normal maximum of five years. The extension was carried out due to World War I. This Act was repealed by the Statute Law Revision Act, 1927.

British North America Act, 1930

Further information: Natural Resources Transfer Acts

Gave the newer provinces of British Columbia, Alberta, Manitoba, and Saskatchewan rights over certain natural resources found in Federally-controlled lands. In 1982, this Act was renamed the *Constitution Act, 1930.*

British North America Act, 1940

This act gave the Federal government jurisdiction over Unemployment Insurance thus allowing such a program to be established on a national level. An earlier attempt to create an Unemployment Insurance program during the Great Depression had been ruled to be unconstitutional, since unemployment assistance was judged by the courts to be a provincial responsibility. In 1982, this Act was renamed the *Constitution Act, 1940.*

British North America Act, 1943

This Act delayed redistribution of seats in the Canadian House of Commons until the end of World War II. This Act was repealed in 1982, as being completely outdated and obsolete.

British North America Act, 1946

This Act adjusted the formula for distributing seats in the Canadian House of Commons among the provinces and territories. This Act was repealed in 1982, as having been superseded.

British North America Act, 1949

See also: Newfoundland Act and 1949 in Canada

This Act allowed for the entry of Newfoundland into the Federation of Canada as its tenth Province. This Act was renamed the **Newfoundland Act** when the Canadian Constitution was patriated from the United Kingdom in 1982.

This Act should not be confused with the British North America (No. 2) Act 1949 (see below).

British North America (No. 2) Act, 1949

This Act granted Canada limited powers to amend its own constitution. The Parliament of Canada was thereafter allowed to amend the Canadian constitution *in many areas of its own jurisdiction* without first obtaining the consent of the British Parliament. However, the approval of the British Parliament was still needed for wider constitutional changes, such as those involving areas of provincial and Federal responsibilities. Therefore, this Act can at best be considered a "partial patriation" of the Canadian Constitution.

This Act was repealed in 1982 with the full patriation of the Canadian Constitution from the United Kingdom, and with the incorporation of a new, comprehensive procedure for amending the Constitution.

This Act is not to be confused with the British North America Act, 1949 - later renamed the Newfoundland Act in 1982 - which confirmed the terms of union between Newfoundland and Canada and which made Newfoundland the tenth province.

British North America Act, 1951

This Act gave the Federal government the power to pass legislation concerning Old Age Pensions, while also recognizing the rights of provincial legislatures to do so. While the Canadian Parliament had established an Old Age Pension program in 1927, this was administered by the provinces and jointly funded by them. This Act of the British Parliament allowed the Federal government of Canada to administer and operate its own pension plan and allowed it to pass the *Old Age Security Act*. This Act was repealed in 1982, since it had been superseded.

British North America Act, 1952

This was the first of the British North America Acts to be enacted by the Canadian Parliament (rather than by the British Parliament). That had been made possible under the provisions of the British North America (No. 2) Act, 1949.

This Act changed the number of seats in the House of Commons and it also limited the number of seats that a province could lose due to redistricting based on the national census to 15% of its previous number of seats. Thus Act also gave the Yukon Territory its own Member of Parliament. This Act was repealed in 1982 as having become obsolete and superseded.

British North America Act, 1960

This Act instituted a mandatory retirement age of 75 for all superior court judges. In 1982, this Act was renamed the *Constitution Act, 1960.*

British North America Act, 1964

This Act extended the Federal government's jurisdiction over pensions to include those of survivor's benefits and disability benefits while continuing to allow the Provinces to have their own pension programs. This amendment to the BNA Act made the Canada Pension Plan possible. In 1982, this Act was renamed the *Constitution Act, 1964.*

British North America Act, 1965

This was the second of the British North America Acts to be enacted by the Parliament of Canada. This was made possible by the provisions of the British North America (No. 2) Act, 1949.

In 1982, this Act was renamed the **Constitution Act, 1965**. It was introduced by the government of Prime Minister Lester B. Pearson, and it established a mandatory retirement age of 75 for all members who had been appointed to the Canadian Senate. Those who had been appointed before the passage of this Act were exempted.

British North America Act, 1974

This was the third of the British North America Acts to be enacted by the Parliament of Canada. This had been made possible by the provisions of the British North America (No. 2) Act, 1949.

This Act changed the rules for the redistribution of seats in the Canadian House of Commons so that Quebec was allocated the fixed number of 75 seats, while other the number of seats allocated to each of the other provinces would always be determined based upon the sizes of their populations in comparison with that of Quebec. However, the Provinces continued to be guaranteed to have at least as many members of the House of Commons as Senators they had in Senators. In 1982, this Act was renamed the *Constitution Act, 1974.*

British North America Act, 1975

This was the fourth of the British North America Acts to be enacted by the Parliament of Canada. This had been made possible by the provisions of the British North America (No. 2) Act, 1949.

Thus Act increased the number of representative from the Northwest Territories in the Canadian House of Commons, from one to two members. In 1982, this Act was renamed the *Constitution Act (No. 1), 1975*.

British North America Act (No. 2), 1975

This was the fifth of the British North America Acts to be enacted by the Parliament of Canada.

This Act increased the number of seats in the Canadian Senate from 102 to 104, and it allocated one seat to the Yukon Territory and one to the Northwest Territories. In 1982, this Act was renamed the *Constitution Act (No. 2), 1975*.

Canada Act, 1982

Main article: Canada Act, 1982

This final Act of the British Parliament regarding Canada had a different name, since it renamed all of the previous, unrepealed British North America Acts, amended some of them, and repealed all others, patriated all remaining legislative and constitutional powers to Canada, and included the Constitution Act, 1982 as its schedule.

External links

- The original acts cited below are held by the Parliamentary Archives.
- Texts on Wikisource:
  - British North America Act, 1867
  - British North America Act, 1871
  - British North America Act, 1886
  - British North America Act, 1907
  - British North America Act, 1915
  - British North America Act, 1916
  - British North America Act, 1930
  - British North America Act, 1940
  - British North America Act, 1943
  - British North America Act, 1946
  - British North America Act, 1949
  - British North America (No. 2) Act, 1949
  - British North America Act, 1951

- British North America Act, 1952
- British North America Act, 1960
- British North America Act, 1964
- British North America Act, 1965
- British North America Act, 1974
- British North America Act, 1975
- British North America Act (No. 2), 1975

Bank of Canada

Bank of Canada

Bank of Canada Banque du Canada	
 The Bank of Canada Building in Ottawa.	
Headquarters	Ottawa, Ontario, Canada
Coordinates	45°25′15″N 75°42′11″W
Established	1935
Governor	Mark Carney
Central bank of	Canada
Currency	Canadian dollar
ISO 4217 Code	CAD
Reserves	78.3 billion in assets (2008)
Base borrowing rate	1.75%
Website	www.bankofcanada.ca [1]

The **Bank of Canada** (in French: ***Banque du Canada***) is Canada's central bank. It was created by the Bank of Canada Act of 1934, a law giving it a monopoly on the issuance of banknotes. How much money it creates influences the value of the Canadian dollar. Its stated purpose is to "promote the economic and financial well-being of Canada."

The bank's headquarters are located in the Bank of Canada Building at the corner of Wellington and Bank Streets in downtown Ottawa.

History

See also: Early Canadian banking system

For many years, Canada did not have a central bank. Each of the nation's large banks issued its own currency and there was little government regulation of the nation's money supply. The federal finance department only issued small and very large denomination bank notes ($5 and under, and $500 and higher.) The Bank of Montreal, then the nation's largest bank, acted as the government's banker. Canada, with its extensive branch banking, had a very stable banking system. There was deemed to be little need for a lender of last resort and the banking system was not hit by the same seasonal liquidity problems as banks in the US. The banking system was regulated by the Canadian Bankers Association that worked in close concert with the government.

While there were some advocates for a central bank in the early part of the twentieth century, most notably bankers and the government, the status quo remained unaltered. This changed with the onset of Great Depression. Many in Canada blamed the policies of the Canadian banks for aggravating the Depression. The money supply was contracting and deflation was common, as the economy corrected from the high inflation in the 1920s. The government claimed it was constrained by its foreign debts, and it would be less costly to borrow money if it could be repaid in debased currency. A major proponent was the Royal Bank of Canada, which wanted to see the government business taken away from the rival Bank of Montreal. The government also claimed it was constrained by its inability to deal directly with its foreign debts. The farmers were joined by manufacturing interests and other groups in favor of a depreciating currency, all demanding a central bank.

Prime Minister R.B. Bennett called a Royal Commission in 1933 and it reported in favour of a central bank. Its members consisted of Britain's chief propagandist during World War I, Lord Macmillan, who supported central banking, as well as various British and Canadian bankers. Gerald Grattan McGeer was one of the most forceful voices in Canada advocating government intervention in the monetary system and nationalizing the credit system. His vision of monetary reform predated the establishment of the Bank of Canada. Also involved was John Edward Brownlee, then Premier of Alberta, petitioning in favor of a central bank because western farmers wanted cheap credit.

The bank began operations on March 11, 1935, after the passage of the Bank of Canada Act. Initially the bank was founded as a privately owned corporation in order to ensure it was free from political influence. In 1938, under Prime Minister William Lyon Mackenzie King, it became " *a special type of* " Crown corporation, fully owned by the government; thus, in effect, by the Canadian taxpayers; with the governor appointed by Cabinet. The responsibility for creating small bills was transferred from the finance department and the private banks were ordered to remove their currency from circulation by 1949. It is important to distinguish between the right to "issue money", which is the sole right of the Bank of Canada, and the ability to "create money", which, through legislation and regulation enacted by Parliament, is largely done by commercial banks through the taking of deposits and the issuance of loans; presently, the Bank of Canada "issues" less than 5% of Canada's money, more than 95% of

Canada's money is "created" by commercial banks, bearing interest, through the process of fractional-reserve banking.

The bank played an important role in financing Canada's war effort during World War II by printing money and buying the government's debt. After the war, the bank's role was expanded as it was mandated to encourage economic growth in Canada. The subsidiary Industrial Development Bank was formed to stimulate investment in Canadian businesses. The monetary policy of the bank was geared towards increasing the money supply to cause low interest rates, and have full employment with little concern about rising prices. When inflation began to rise in the early 1960s, the governor James Coyne ordered a reduction in the money supply. Prime Minister John Diefenbaker disagreed with this move, and ordered a return to the full-employment policies. Since the 1980s, keeping inflation low has been its main priority. The bank's Ottawa headquarters building is the site of the Currency Museum, which opened in December 1980.

Roles and responsibilities

The principal role of the Bank of Canada, as defined in the Bank of Canada Act, is "to promote the economic and financial welfare of Canada." The bank's current mission statement is:

> *The Bank of Canada's responsibilities focus on the goals of low and stable inflation, a safe and secure currency, financial stability, and the efficient management of government funds and public debt.*

In practice, however, it has a more narrow and specific internal definition of that mandate: to keep the rate of inflation between 1% and 3% by printing a certain amount of money. Since the Bank's creation, the Canadian dollar has had an average annual inflation rate of 3.14%. The only tool the Bank of Canada has to achieve this goal is its ability to set the interest rate for borrowed money. At one time the Bank of Canada could dictate the amount of reserves that Canadian chartered banks must keep but that power was removed in the early 1990s.

Since 1998, the Bank's policy has been to intervene in the foreign exchange market only under exceptional circumstances. In this sense, the Canadian dollar's value is determined by the market supply and demand for Canadian currency.

Type of government institution

The Bank is not a government department as it performs its activities at arm's-length from the government; it is claimed to be a Crown corporation owned by the Government. Shares are directly held by the Ministry of Finance, and the bank's earnings go into the federal treasury. The Governor and Senior Deputy Governor are appointed by the Bank's Board of Directors. The Deputy Minister of Finance sits on the Board of Directors but does not have a vote. The Bank submits its spending to the Board of Directors, while federal departments submit their spending estimates to the Treasury Board.

Its employees are regulated by the Bank and not the federal public service agencies. Its books are audited by external auditors who are appointed by Cabinet on the recommendation of the Minister of Finance, not by the Auditor General of Canada.

Governor

The head of the Bank of Canada is the Governor, who is appointed by the Bank's Board of Directors. The Governor is appointed for a seven-year term, and can be dismissed by the government. In case of a profound disagreement between the government and the Bank, the Minister of Finance can issue written instructions for the Bank to change its policies. This has never actually happened in the history of the Bank to date. In practice, the Governor sets monetary policy independently of the government.

Bank of Canada Governors

- Mark Carney (2008-Present)
- David A. Dodge (2001–2008)
- Gordon Thiessen (1994–2001)
- John Crow (1987–1994)
- Gerald Bouey (1973–1987)
- Louis Rasminsky (1961–1973)
- James Coyne (1955–1961)
- Graham Towers (1934–1954)

See also

- Canadian dollar
- List of banks in Canada

References

- George S. Watts *Bank of Canada/La Banque du Canada: Origines et premieres annees/Origins and Early History* McGill-Queen's University Press
- James Powell *The Bank of Canada of James Elliot Coyne: Challenges, Confrontation, and Change* McGill-Queen's University Press September 23, 2009

External links

- (English) (French) Bank of Canada official site [1]
- Bank of Canada Act [B-2] [1]

Central bank

A **central bank**, **reserve bank**, or **monetary authority** is a banking institution granted the exclusive privilege to lend a government its currency. Like a normal commercial bank, a central bank charges interest on the loans made to borrowers, primarily the government of whichever country the bank exists for, and to other commercial banks, typically as a 'lender of last resort'. However, a central bank is distinguished from a normal commercial bank because it has a monopoly on creating the currency of that nation, which is loaned to the government in the form of legal tender. It is a bank that can lend money to other banks in times of need.

Its primary function is to provide the nation's money supply, but more active duties include controlling subsidized-loan interest rates, and acting as a lender of last resort to the banking sector during times of financial crisis (private banks often being integral to the national financial system). It may also have supervisory powers, to ensure that banks and other financial institutions do not behave recklessly or fraudulently.

Most of the rich countries today have an "independent" central bank, that is, one which operates under rules designed to prevent political interference. Examples include the European Central Bank (ECB) and the Federal Reserve System in the United States. Some central banks are publicly owned, and others are privately owned. The United States Federal Reserve "is an unusual mixture of public and private elements".

History

In Europe prior to the 17th century most money was commodity money, typically gold or silver. However, promises to pay were widely circulated and accepted as value at least five hundred years earlier in both Europe and Asia. The Song Dynasty was the first to issue generally circulating paper currency, while the Yuan Dynasty was the first to use notes as the predominant circulating medium. In 1455, in an effort to control inflation, the succeeding Ming Dynasty ended the use of paper money and closed much of Chinese trade. The medieval European Knights Templar ran an early prototype of a central banking system, as their promises to pay were widely respected, and many regard their activities as having laid the basis for the modern banking system.

As the first public bank to "offer accounts not directly convertible to coin", the Bank of Amsterdam established in 1609 is considered to be a precursor to a central bank. In 1664, the central bank of

Sweden—"Sveriges Riksbank" or simply "Riksbanken"—was founded in Stockholm and is by that the world's oldest central bank (still operating today). This was followed in 1694 by the Bank of England, created by Scottish businessman William Paterson in the City of London at the request of the English government to help pay for a war.

Although central banks today are generally associated with fiat money, the nineteenth and early twentieth centuries central banks in most of Europe and Japan developed under the international gold standard, elsewhere free banking or currency boards were more usual at this time. Problems with collapses of banks during downturns, however, was leading to wider support for central banks in those nations which did not as yet possess them, most notably in Australia.

With the collapse of the gold standard after World War I, central banks became much more widespread. The US Federal Reserve was created by the U.S. Congress through the passing of the Glass-Owen Bill, signed by President Woodrow Wilson on December 23, 1913, whilst Australia established its first central bank in 1920, Colombia in 1923, Mexico and Chile in 1925 and Canada and New Zealand in the aftermath of the Great Depression in 1934. By 1935, the only significant independent nation that did not possess a central bank was Brazil, which developed a precursor thereto in 1945 and created its present central bank twenty years later. When African and Asian countries gained independence, all of them rapidly established central banks or monetary unions.

The People's Bank of China evolved its role as a central bank starting in about 1979 with the introduction of market reforms in that country, and this accelerated in 1989 when the country took a generally capitalist approach to developing at least its export economy. By 2000 the People's Bank of China was in all senses a modern central bank, and emerged as such partly in response to the European Central Bank. This is the most modern bank model and was introduced with the euro to coordinate the European national banks, which continue to separately manage their respective economies other than currency exchange and base interest rates.

Activities and responsibilities

Functions of a central bank (not all functions are carried out by all banks):

- implementing monetary policy
- determining Interest rates
- controlling the nation's entire money supply
- the Government's banker and the bankers' bank ("lender of last resort")
- managing the country's foreign exchange and gold reserves and the Government's stock register
- regulating and supervising the banking industry
- setting the official interest rate – used to manage both inflation and the country's exchange rate – and ensuring that this rate takes effect via a variety of policy mechanisms

Monetary policy

The Bank of England, central bank of the United Kingdom

Central banks implement a country's chosen monetary policy. At the most basic level, this involves establishing what form of currency the country may have, whether a fiat currency, gold-backed currency (disallowed for countries with membership of the IMF), currency board or a currency union. When a country has its own national currency, this involves the issue of some form of standardized currency, which is essentially a form of promissory note: a promise to exchange the note for "money" under certain circumstances. Historically, this was often a promise to exchange the money for precious metals in some fixed amount. Now, when many currencies are fiat money, the "promise to pay" consists of nothing more than a promise to pay the same sum in the same currency.

The Bank of Canada

In many countries, the central bank may use another country's currency either directly (in a currency union), or indirectly, by using a currency board. In the latter case, local currency is directly backed by the central bank's holdings of a foreign currency in a fixed-ratio; this mechanism is used, notably, in Bulgaria, Hong Kong and Estonia.

In countries with fiat money, monetary policy may be used as a shorthand form for the interest rate targets and other active measures undertaken by the monetary authority.

Goals of monetary policy

Price Stability

Unanticipated inflation leads to lender losses. Nominal contracts attempt to account for inflation. Effort successful if monetary policy able to maintain steady rate of inflation.

High Employment

The movement of workers between jobs is referred to as frictional unemployment. All unemployment beyond frictional unemployment is classified as unintended unemployment. Reduction in this area is the target of macroeconomic policy.

Economic Growth

Economic growth is enhanced by investment in technological advances in production. Encouragement of savings supplies funds that can be drawn upon for investment.

Interest Rate Stability

Volatile interest and exchange rates generate costs to lenders and borrowers. Unexpected changes that cause damage, making policy formulation difficult.

Financial Market Stability

Foreign Exchange Market Stability

Conflicts Among Goals

Goals frequently cannot be separated from each other and often conflict. Costs must therefore be carefully weighed before policy implementation. To make conflict productive, to turn it into an opportunity for change and progress, Follett advises against domination, manipulation, or compromise. "Just so far as people think that the basis of working together is compromise or concession, just so far they do not understand the first principles of working together. Such people think that when they have reached an appreciation of the necessity of compromise they have reached a high plane of social development . . . But compromise is still on the same plane as fighting. War will continue - between capital and labour, between nation and nation - until we reliquich the ideas of compromise and concession."

Currency issuance

United States Federal Reserve

Many central banks are "banks" in the sense that they hold assets (foreign exchange, gold, and other financial assets) and liabilities. A central bank's primary liabilities are the currency outstanding, and these liabilities are backed by the assets the bank owns.

Central banks generally earn money by issuing currency notes and "selling" them to the public for interest-bearing assets, such as government bonds. Since currency usually pays no interest, the difference in interest generates income, called seigniorage. In most central banking systems, this income is remitted to the government. The European Central Bank remits its interest income to its owners, the central banks of the member countries of the European Union.

Although central banks generally hold government debt, in some countries the outstanding amount of government debt is smaller than the amount the central bank may wish to hold. In many countries, central banks may hold significant amounts of foreign currency assets, rather than assets in their own national currency, particularly when the national currency is fixed to other currencies.

Naming of central banks

There is no standard terminology for the name of a central bank, but many countries use the "Bank of Country" form (e.g., Bank of England, Bank of Canada, Bank of Russia). Some are styled "national" banks, such as the National Bank of Ukraine; but the term "national bank" is more often used by privately-owned commercial banks, especially in the United States. In other cases, central banks may incorporate the word "Central" (e.g. European Central Bank, Central Bank of Ireland). The word "Reserve" is also often included, such as the Reserve Bank of India, Reserve Bank of Australia, Reserve Bank of New Zealand, the South African Reserve Bank, and U.S. Federal Reserve System. Many countries have state-owned banks or other quasi-government entities that have entirely separate functions, such as financing imports and exports.

In some countries, particularly in some Communist countries, the term national bank may be used to indicate both the monetary authority and the leading banking entity, such as the USSR's Gosbank (state bank). In other countries, the term national bank may be used to indicate that the central bank's goals are broader than monetary stability, such as full employment, industrial development, or other goals.

Interest rate interventions

Typically a central bank controls certain types of short-term interest rates. These influence the stock- and bond markets as well as mortgage and other interest rates. The European Central Bank for example announces its interest rate at the meeting of its Governing Council; in the case of the Federal Reserve, the Board of Governors.

Both the Federal Reserve and the ECB are composed of one or more central bodies that are responsible for the main decisions about interest rates and the size and type of open market operations, and several branches to execute its policies. In the case of the Fed, they are the local Federal Reserve Banks; for the ECB they are the national central banks.

Limits of enforcement power

Central Bank of Brazil in Brasília

Contrary to popular perception, central banks are not all-powerful and have limited powers to put their policies into effect. Most importantly, although the perception by the public may be that the "central bank" controls some or all interest rates and currency rates, economic theory (and substantial empirical evidence) shows that it is impossible to do both at once in an open economy. Robert Mundell's "impossible trinity" is the most famous formulation of these limited powers, and postulates that it is impossible to target monetary policy (broadly, interest rates), the exchange rate (through a fixed rate) and maintain free capital movement. Since most Western economies are now considered "open" with free capital movement, this essentially means that central banks may target interest rates or exchange rates with credibility, but not both at once.

Even when targeting interest rates, most central banks have limited ability to influence the rates actually paid by private individuals and companies. In the most famous case of policy failure, George Soros arbitraged the pound sterling's relationship to the ECU and (after making $2 billion himself and forcing the UK to spend over $8bn defending the pound) forced it to abandon its policy. Since then he has been a harsh critic of clumsy bank policies and argued that no one should be able to do what he did.

The most complex relationships are those between the yuan and the US dollar, and between the euro and its neighbours. The situation in Cuba is so exceptional as to require the Cuban peso to be dealt with simply as an exception, since the United States forbids direct trade with Cuba. US dollars were ubiquitous in Cuba's economy after its legalization in 1991, but were officially removed from circulation in 2004 and replaced by the convertible peso.

Policy instruments

Bank of Israel

The main monetary policy instruments available to central banks are open market operation, bank reserve requirement, interest rate policy, re-lending and re-discount (including using the term repurchase market), and credit policy (often coordinated with trade policy). While capital adequacy is important, it is defined and regulated by the Bank for International Settlements, and central banks in practice generally do not apply stricter rules.

To enable open market operations, a central bank must hold foreign exchange reserves (usually in the form of government bonds) and official gold reserves. It will often have some influence over any official or mandated exchange rates: Some exchange rates are managed, some are market based (free float) and many are somewhere in between ("managed float" or "dirty float").

Interest rates

By far the most visible and obvious power of many modern central banks is to influence market interest rates; contrary to popular belief, they rarely "set" rates to a fixed number. Although the mechanism differs from country to country, most use a similar mechanism based on a central bank's ability to create as much fiat money as required.

The mechanism to move the market towards a 'target rate' (whichever specific rate is used) is generally to lend money or borrow money in theoretically unlimited quantities, until the targeted market rate is sufficiently close to the target. Central banks may do so by lending money to and borrowing money from (taking deposits from) a limited number of qualified banks, or by purchasing and selling bonds. As an example of how this functions, the Bank of Canada sets a target overnight rate, and a band of plus or minus 0.25%. Qualified banks borrow from each other within this band, but never above or below, because the central bank will always lend to them at the top of the band, and take deposits at the bottom of the band; in principle, the capacity to borrow and lend at the extremes of the band are unlimited. Other central banks use similar mechanisms.

It is also notable that the target rates are generally short-term rates. The actual rate that borrowers and lenders receive on the market will depend on (perceived) credit risk, maturity and other factors. For example, a central bank might set a target rate for overnight lending of 4.5%, but rates for (equivalent risk) five-year bonds might be 5%, 4.75%, or, in cases of inverted yield curves, even below the short-term rate. Many central banks have one primary "headline" rate that is quoted as the "central bank rate." In practice, they will have other tools and rates that are used, but only one that is rigorously targeted and enforced.

"The rate at which the central bank lends money can indeed be chosen at will by the central bank; this is the rate that makes the financial headlines." - Henry C.K. Liu. Liu explains further that "the U.S. central-bank lending rate is known as the Fed funds rate. The Fed sets a target for the Fed funds rate, which its Open Market Committee tries to match by lending or borrowing in the money market ... a fiat money system set by command of the central bank. The Fed is the head of the central-bank because the U.S. dollar is the key reserve currency for international trade. The global money market is a USA dollar market. All other currencies markets revolve around the U.S. dollar market." Accordingly the U.S. situation is not typical of central banks in general.

A typical central bank has several interest rates or monetary policy tools it can set to influence markets.

- Marginal lending rate (currently 1.75% in the Eurozone) – a fixed rate for institutions to borrow money from the central bank. (In the USA this is called the discount rate).
- Main refinancing rate (1.00% in the Eurozone) – the publicly visible interest rate the central bank announces. It is also known as *minimum bid rate* and serves as a bidding floor for refinancing loans. (In the USA this is called the federal funds rate).
- Deposit rate (0.25% in the Eurozone) – the rate parties receive for deposits at the central bank.

These rates directly affect the rates in the money market, the market for short term loans.

Open market operations

Through open market operations, a central bank influences the money supply in an economy directly. Each time it buys securities, exchanging money for the security, it raises the money supply. Conversely, selling of securities lowers the money supply. Buying of securities thus amounts to printing new money while lowering supply of the specific security.

The main open market operations are:

- Temporary lending of money for collateral securities ("Reverse Operations" or "repurchase operations", otherwise known as the "repo" market). These operations are carried out on a regular basis, where fixed maturity loans (of 1 week and 1 month for the ECB) are auctioned off.
- Buying or selling securities ("direct operations") on ad-hoc basis.
- Foreign exchange operations such as forex swaps.

All of these interventions can also influence the foreign exchange market and thus the exchange rate. For example the People's Bank of China and the Bank of Japan have on occasion bought several hundred billions of U.S. Treasuries, presumably in order to stop the decline of the U.S. dollar versus the renminbi and the yen.

Capital requirements

All banks are required to hold a certain percentage of their assets as capital, a rate which may be established by the central bank or the banking supervisor. For international banks, including the 55 member central banks of the Bank for International Settlements, the threshold is 8% (see the Basel Capital Accords) of risk-adjusted assets, whereby certain assets (such as government bonds) are considered to have lower risk and are either partially or fully excluded from total assets for the purposes of calculating capital adequacy. Partly due to concerns about asset inflation and repurchase agreements, capital requirements may be considered more effective than deposit/reserve requirements in preventing indefinite lending: when at the threshold, a bank cannot extend another loan without acquiring further capital on its balance sheet.

Reserve requirements

In practice, many banks are required to hold a percentage of their deposits as reserves. Such legal reserve requirements were introduced in the nineteenth century to reduce the risk of banks overextending themselves and suffering from bank runs, as this could lead to knock-on effects on other banks. *See also money multiplier.* As the early 20th century gold standard and late 20th century dollar hegemony evolved, and as banks proliferated and engaged in more complex transactions and were able to profit from dealings globally on a moment's notice, these practices became mandatory, if only to ensure that there was some limit on the ballooning of money supply. Such limits have become harder to enforce. The People's Bank of China retains (and uses) more powers over reserves because the yuan that it manages is a non-convertible currency.

Even if reserves were not a legal requirement, prudence would ensure that banks would hold a certain percentage of their assets in the form of cash reserves. It is common to think of commercial banks as passive receivers of deposits from their customers and, for many purposes, this is still an accurate view.

This passive view of bank activity is misleading when it comes to considering what determines the nation's money supply and credit. Loan activity by banks plays a fundamental role in determining the money supply. The central-bank money after aggregate settlement - **final money** - can take only one of two forms:

- physical cash, which is rarely used in wholesale financial markets,
- central-bank money.

The currency component of the money supply is far smaller than the deposit component. Currency and bank reserves together make up the monetary base, called M1 and M2.

Exchange requirements

To influence the money supply, some central banks may require that some or all foreign exchange receipts (generally from exports) be exchanged for the local currency. The rate that is used to purchase local currency may be market-based or arbitrarily set by the bank. This tool is generally used in countries with non-convertible currencies or partially-convertible currencies. The recipient of the local currency may be allowed to freely dispose of the funds, required to hold the funds with the central bank for some period of time, or allowed to use the funds subject to certain restrictions. In other cases, the ability to hold or use the foreign exchange may be otherwise limited.

In this method, money supply is increased by the central bank when it purchases the foreign currency by issuing (selling) the local currency. The central bank may subsequently reduce the money supply by various means, including selling bonds or foreign exchange interventions.

Margin requirements and other tools

In some countries, central banks may have other tools that work indirectly to limit lending practices and otherwise restrict or regulate capital markets. For example, a central bank may regulate margin lending, whereby individuals or companies may borrow against pledged securities. The margin requirement establishes a minimum ratio of the value of the securities to the amount borrowed.

Central banks often have requirements for the quality of assets that may be held by financial institutions; these requirements may act as a limit on the amount of risk and leverage created by the financial system. These requirements may be direct, such as requiring certain assets to bear certain minimum credit ratings, or indirect, by the central bank lending to counterparties only when security of a certain quality is pledged as collateral.

Examples of use

The People's Bank of China has been forced into particularly aggressive and differentiating tactics by the extreme complexity and rapid expansion of the economy it manages. It imposed some absolute restrictions on lending to specific industries in 2003, and continues to require 1% more (7%) reserves from urban banks (typically focusing on export) than rural ones. This is not by any means an unusual situation. The USA historically had very wide ranges of reserve requirements between its dozen branches. Domestic development is thought to be optimized mostly by reserve requirements rather than by capital adequacy methods, since they can be more finely tuned and regionally varied.

Banking supervision and other activities

Finance

In some countries a central bank through its subsidiaries controls and monitors the banking sector. In other countries banking supervision is carried out by a government department such as the UK Treasury, or an independent government agency (e.g. UK's Financial Services Authority). It examines the banks' balance sheets and behaviour and policies toward consumers. Apart from refinancing, it also provides banks with services such as transfer of funds, bank notes and coins or foreign currency. Thus it is often described as the "bank of banks".

Many countries such as the United States will monitor and control the banking sector through different agencies and for different purposes, although there is usually significant cooperation between the agencies. For example, money center banks, deposit-taking institutions, and other types of financial institutions may be subject to different (and occasionally overlapping) regulation. Some types of banking regulation may be delegated to other levels of government, such as state or provincial governments.

Any cartel of banks is particularly closely watched and controlled. Most countries control bank mergers and are wary of concentration in this industry due to the danger of groupthink and runaway lending bubbles based on a single point of failure, the credit culture of the few large banks.

Independence

Over the past decade, there has been a trend towards increasing the independence of central banks as a way of improving long-term economic performance. However, while a large volume of economic research has been done to define the relationship between central bank independence and economic performance, the results are ambiguous.

Advocates of central bank independence argue that a central bank which is too susceptible to political direction or pressure may encourage economic cycles ("boom and bust"), as politicians may be tempted to boost economic activity in advance of an election, to the detriment of the long-term health of the economy and the country. In this context, independence is usually defined as the central bank's operational and management independence from the government.

The literature on central bank independence has defined a number of types of independence.

Legal independence

> The independence of the central bank is enshrined in law. This type of independence is limited in a democratic state; in almost all cases the central bank is accountable at some level to government officials, either through a government minister or directly to a legislature. Even defining degrees of legal independence has proven to be a challenge since legislation typically

provides only a framework within which the government and the central bank work out their relationship.

Goal independence

The central bank has the right to set its own policy goals, whether inflation targeting, control of the money supply, or maintaining a fixed exchange rate. While this type of independence is more common, many central banks prefer to announce their policy goals in partnership with the appropriate government departments. This increases the transparency of the policy setting process and thereby increases the credibility of the goals chosen by providing assurance that they will not be changed without notice. In addition, the setting of common goals by the central bank and the government helps to avoid situations where monetary and fiscal policy are in conflict; a policy combination that is clearly sub-optimal.

Operational independence

The central bank has the independence to determine the best way of achieving its policy goals, including the types of instruments used and the timing of their use. This is the most common form of central bank independence. The granting of independence to the Bank of England in 1997 was, in fact, the granting of operational independence; the inflation target continued to be announced in the Chancellor's annual budget speech to Parliament.

Management independence

The central bank has the authority to run its own operations (appointing staff, setting budgets, etc.) without excessive involvement of the government. The other forms of independence are not possible unless the central bank has a significant degree of management independence. One of the most common statistical indicators used in the literature as a proxy for central bank independence is the "turn-over-rate" of central bank governors. If a government is in the habit of appointing and replacing the governor frequently, it clearly has the capacity to micro-manage the central bank through its choice of governors.

It is argued that an independent central bank can run a more credible monetary policy, making market expectations more responsive to signals from the central bank. Recently, both the Bank of England (1997) and the European Central Bank have been made independent and follow a set of published inflation targets so that markets know what to expect. Even the People's Bank of China has been accorded great latitude due to the difficulty of problems it faces, though in the People's Republic of China the official role of the bank remains that of a national bank rather than a central bank, underlined by the official refusal to "unpeg" the yuan or to revalue it "under pressure". The People's Bank of China's independence can thus be read more as independence from the USA which rules the financial markets, than from the Communist Party of China which rules the country. The fact that the Communist Party is not elected also relieves the pressure to please people, increasing its independence.

Governments generally have some degree of influence over even "independent" central banks; the aim of independence is primarily to prevent short-term interference. For example, the chairman of the U.S. Federal Reserve Bank is appointed by the President of the U.S. (all nominees for this post are recommended by the owners of the Federal Reserve, as are all the board members), and his choice must be confirmed by the Congress.

International organizations such as the World Bank, the BIS and the IMF are strong supporters of central bank independence. This results, in part, from a belief in the intrinsic merits of increased independence. The support for independence from the international organizations also derives partly from the connection between increased independence for the central bank and increased transparency in the policy-making process. The IMF's FSAP review self-assessment, for example, includes a number of questions about central bank independence in the transparency section. An independent central bank will score higher in the review than one that is not independent.

Criticism

According to the Austrian School of Economics, central banking plays an important role in business cycles, according to the Austrian Business Cycle Theory. Hayek and Mises both were able to predict The Great Depression. The main proponents of the Austrian business cycle theory are Ludwig von Mises, Friedrich Hayek and Murray Rothbard. F. A. Hayek shared a Nobel Prize in economics (with Stockholm school economist, Gunnar Myrdal) in 1974 based on "their pioneering work in the theory of money" among other contributions. Hayek discusses central banking in his book, The Use of Knowledge in Society.

Alternatives

Demurrage currencies provide an alternative and perhaps complementary means towards central banking's goal of sustaining economic growth with different specific characteristics and a mechanism that follows naturally from the use of commodity currencies, is more uniform in operation, does not devalue the currency unit, and is more predictable and potentially more decentralized in its operation. Historically, the idea of demurrage influenced Keynes' prescription for net-inflationary central bank policy.

See also

- Capitol Hill Baby-Sitting Co-op
- Fractional-reserve banking
- List of central banks
- National bank
- Seigniorage
- State bank

References

"*Genoa and the history of finance: a series of firsts ?*" Giuseppe Felloni, Guido Laura. 9 November 2004, ISBN 88-87822-16-6 (book can be downloaded at giuseppefelloni.it)

External links

- A Central Bank as a Menace to Liberty, by George H. Earle, Jr.—Philadelphia lawyer and businessman. (1908)
- Interactive map of all the central banks [1]
- The Federal Reserve System: Purposes and Functions [2]-- A publication of the U.S. Federal Reserve, describing its role in the macroeconomy
- The Federal Reserve in Plain English—An easy-to-read guide to the structure and functions of the Federal Reserve System [3]
- The Eurosystem [4]-- Website of the European Central Bank describing the structure of the central banking system in the Eurozone
- *A hundred ways to skin a cat: comparing monetary policy operating procedures in the United States, Japan and the euro area* [5]PDF (176 KB) - C E V Borio, Bank for International Settlements, Basel
- *Banking Bunkum: A critique of the role of central banks around the world* [6] - Henry C K Liu
- VB.com Central Banks [7] - Addresses and Phone numbers of all Central Banks
- List of central bank websites at the Bank for International Settlements [8]
- Seigniorage [9] - List of central banks worldwide with links
- Cbrates.com: Worldwide Central Bank Rates [10]
- Centralbanks UN nations A-M [11]
- Centralbanks UN nations N-Ö [12]
- Centralbanks Non UN nations/territories [13]

Bank of Canada Building

The **Bank of Canada Building** is the head office of the Bank of Canada, located in Ottawa, Ontario, Canada.

The Bank of Canada Building in Ottawa.

Built from 1937-1938 by architect S.G. Davenport of Montreal and completed by the Toronto firm of Marani, Lawson and Morris, it replaced the Victoria Building to the east of this building on Wellington Street. Constructed of grey granite from Quebec, it is late neoclassical in style, which was very popular at the time among banks, and won a number of architectural awards, including the Gold Medal from the Royal Architectural Institute of Canada.

The large bronze front doors were designed by Ulysses Ricci of New York, and decorated with facsimiles of Greek coins from the British Museum. The sculptures decorating the front facade were designed by Jacobine Jones, and represent the Canada's seven principal industries at the time: fishing, electricity, mining, agriculture, forestry, manufacturing, and construction. The cornerstone was placed by Prime Minister Mackenzie King and the Bank's first governor, Graham Towers.

Plans for additions in the 1940s and 1950s were scrapped, and while more substantial plans were drafted during the 1960s, construction was delayed due to Ottawa's already-strained construction industry, and only commenced in 1972. The glass structure behind the original 1937 structure was completed in 1979 by the firm Marani Rounthwaite & Dick (successor to Marani, Lawson and Morris) and Arthur Erickson. The building contains an enclosed courtyard with a large tropical garden bordering a shallow pool which is very popular with wedding photographers, and a three-ton Yap Stone.

In 2000, it was named by the Royal Architectural Institute of Canada as one of the top 500 buildings produced in Canada during the last millennium.

External links

- Bank of Canada HQ [1]

Geographical coordinates: 45°25′15″N 75°42′10″W

The "Big Five" Banks

Big Five (banks)

Big Five is the name colloquially given to the five biggest banks that dominate the banking industry in Canada. All five banks are operationally headquartered in Toronto, Ontario.

The Big Five Banks are all classified as Schedule I banks that are domestic banks operating in Canada under government charter. The banks' shares are widely held, with any entity allowed to hold a maximum of twenty percent.

Overview

The Big Five banks, listed in order of market capitalization on the TSX (largest to smallest, as of December 31st, 2009) with their current corporate brand names and corporate profiles (according to their respective 2009 Annual Reports, all monetary amounts are in billions C$), are:

Official names	Bank brand	Headquarters	Assets	Deposits	Capitalization	Branches (Canada only)	Employees (Full-time equivalent)	Reference
Royal Bank of Canada Banque Royale du Canada	RBC Royal Bank RBC Banque Royale	Toronto (operational) Montreal (legal)	$655.0	$398.2	$75.5	**1,197**	**71,186**	
Toronto-Dominion Bank Banque Toronto-Dominion	TD Canada Trust	Toronto	$557.2	$391.0	$56.7	**1,116**	**65,930**	
Bank of Nova Scotia Banque de Nouvelle-Écosse	Scotiabank Banque Scotia	Toronto (operational) Halifax (domicile)	$496.5	$350.4	$48.8	**1,019**	**67,802**	
Bank of Montreal Banque de Montréal	BMO Bank of Montreal BMO Banque de Montréal	Toronto (operational) Montreal (legal)	$388.5	$236.2	$31.0	**900**	**36,173**	

Canadian Imperial Bank of Commerce Banque Canadienne Impériale de Commerce	CIBC	Toronto	$335.9	$223.1	$26.2	**1,072**	**41,941**	

In modern history, Royal Bank has always been the largest by a significant margin. Up to the late 1990s, CIBC was the second largest, followed by Bank of Montreal, Scotiabank, and TD Bank. During the late 1990s and beyond, this ranking changed due to several reorganizations. Royal Bank acquired Royal Trust, then the second-largest trust in Canada, in 1993, while Scotiabank purchased National Trust in 1997. As Scotiabank found no merger partners among the other banks in the big five group, it instead expanded its international operations and passed the Bank of Montreal in size. TD Bank merged with Canada Trust, which was for a long time the largest trust in Canada, thus vaulting TD temporarily into the number two spot. While there were no major changes to Bank of Montreal, CIBC's unsuccessful foray into the US market led it to shed its assets there, dropping it to the number five spot.

The term **Big Six Banks** is frequently used as well. The "Big Six" also includes the National Bank of Canada since historically the bank had a network of over 650 branches. Over the years, more than 200 of them were closed, and although the majority of its operations has always been focused in the province of Quebec, it is even more so now. The Big Six chartered banks participate in the Large Value Transfer System (LVTS) together with eight other banks (including the Bank of Canada).

Other banks with substantial operations in Canada

Official names	**Headquarters**	**Assets**	**Deposits**	**Capitalization**	**Branches (Canada only)**	**Employees (Full-time equivalent)**	**Reference**
National Bank of Canada Banque Nationale du Canada	Montreal	$132.1	$75.2	$9.7	**445**	**14,851**	
HSBC Bank Canada Banque HSBC Canada	Vancouver	$71.3	$50.2		**145**		
Canadian Western Bank	Edmonton	$11.6	$9.6	$1.4	**37**		
Laurentian Bank of Canada Banque Laurentienne du Canada	Montreal	$22.2	$18.3	$1.0	**156**	**3,528**	

Proposed mergers

In 1998, the Bank of Montreal proposed a merger with Royal Bank around the same time that CIBC proposed to combine with the Toronto-Dominion Bank. The banks argued that these mergers would enable them to compete globally with other financial institutions.

This would have left Canada with only three major national banks. Thus, the mergers were reviewed by the Competition Bureau of Canada. The Competition Bureau declared that negative effects (such as higher user fees and local branch closures) from the mergers would far outweigh the benefits of allowing the mergers. Ultimately, it was then Finance Minister Paul Martin who rejected both proposed mergers. The issue since has not been revisited by succeeding Finance Ministers.

Potential foreign forays

The strength of the Canadian dollar and relative weakness of U.S. bank prices have led commentators to suggest that the big five banks could consider an expansion into the United States. The weakness of the Canadian dollar, as well as high U.S. bank stock prices, were commonly cited as obstacles to purchasing assets south of the border.

Due to the recent 2007 Subprime mortgage financial crisis, Royal Bank of Canada has now eclipsed Morgan Stanley in terms of market valuation. According to figures compiled by a recent Bloomberg report, investors today are willing to pay about $2.60 for every dollar of book value at a Canadian bank, compared with $1.70 in the United States. That ratio is about the reverse of where it stood in late 1999.

The last time the U.S. financial markets were weak, many Canadian bank CEOs were criticized for not making a more concerted buying effort. Some believed that these CEOs preferred to wait for Ottawa to bless domestic mergers before expanding into the US. The federal government ended up refusing to allow the mergers, and is unlikely to do so now. Analysts also pointed out that Canadian banks have much stronger balance sheets today than they did 10 or 15 years ago, putting them in an even better position to be aggressive.

In October 2007, TD purchased Commerce Bancorp, a medium sized US bank with a strong branch network in the middle Atlantic and Florida. As of March 2008, their stated plan was to merge Commerce with their existing TD Banknorth subsidiary, calling the new bank TD Commerce Bank. However, the name was challenged by a "Commerce Bank" in New England. As a result, TD will name its US banks to TD Bank by end of 2009. TD is the sixth-largest bank by branch network in North America, after JPMorgan, Bank of America, Wells Fargo, PNC, and US Bank.

Banking Regulation

The new framework includes revised ownership rules for banks and a new size-based ownership regime. Under the previous framework, a distinction was drawn between Schedule I and Schedule II banks (see Annex 1 for a list of these banks). Shares of Schedule I banks were required to be widely held, with no single shareholder or group of shareholders holding more than 10 per cent of any class of shares, while Schedule II banks could be owned by eligible Canadian or foreign financial institutions.

Under the new legislation an individual investor will now be permitted to own up to 20 per cent of any class of voting shares of a widely held bank and up to 30 per cent of any class of non-voting shares, subject only to a "fit and proper" test designed to evaluate the applicant's character and suitability. This will allow widely held banks to enter into strategic alliances and joint ventures involving significant share exchanges. At the same time, the Bank Act will continue to prohibit control of a large financial institution by any single shareholder or group of shareholders. The Government has signalled its intention to issue guidelines that will clarify for investors and institutions the factual criteria and policy objectives to be taken into consideration in assessing control. The Government will be developing these guidelines in consultation with representatives of financial institutions and the broader investment community.

The new framework also enables banks to organize under a regulated holding-company structure that provides them with greater flexibility to compete with large specialized or unregulated firms. Both holding companies and banks structured along the traditional parent-subsidiary model are permitted to have a broader range of investments than under the previous regime.

Furthermore, the previous regime of Schedule I and Schedule II banks is now replaced by a new size-based ownership regime under which:

- large banks (banks with equity in excess of $5 billion) must remain "widely held" as outlined in the new definition;
- medium-sized banks (i.e., banks with equity between $1 billion and $5 billion) are allowed to have individual shareholdings of up to 65 per cent, with at least 35 per cent of voting shares being publicly held; and
- small banks (i.e., banks with equity of less than $1 billion) have no ownership restrictions other than "fit and proper" tests.

The new size-based ownership regime also allows for the creation of community-based banks with services tailored to the needs of a specific clientele. These banks will still be able to compete with the major banks in local or regional markets. The new regime also allows commercial enterprises (for example, those with a significant retail presence) to own a bank.

To encourage competition, the legislation also reduces the minimum capital requirement to start a bank from $10 million to $5 million.

In support of these various initiatives, the policy framework also contains provisions to ensure that financial institutions continue to manage their risks prudently. To this end, the Superintendent of Financial Institutions has been given additional supervisory powers to deal with institutions that do not meet certain supervisory or regulatory requirements. These include the power to remove directors and senior officers of a bank in instances of misconduct, and the power to administer financial penalties against institutions and individuals that do not comply with undertakings or violate the legislation and regulations governing financial institutions.

The framework also includes merger review guidelines that outline a formal and transparent review process for merger proposals between banks with equity in excess of $5 billion. This new process consists of a review of the merger proposal by the Competition Bureau, the Office of the Superintendent of Financial Institutions and the Department of Finance, and of a full public review by the House of Commons Standing Committee on Finance and the Standing Senate Committee on Banking, Trade and Commerce.

Bill C-8 also contains consumer protection measures as well as measures to ensure that the regulatory environment responds to the evolution of the sector in today's rapidly changing marketplace. The Financial Consumer Agency of Canada will be established to enforce the consumer-oriented provisions of the federal financial institution statutes, to monitor the industry's self-regulatory initiatives designed to protect the interests of consumers and small businesses, to promote consumer awareness and to respond to general consumer inquiries. This will consolidate and strengthen existing oversight activities in a dedicated new agency.

A new Canadian Financial Services Ombudsman will also be established to handle consumer and smallbusiness complaints related to dealings with financial institutions. This independent body will operate at arm's-length from government and the financial sector, and a majority of the members of its board of directors will be from outside the financial services sector.

Additional consumer protection measures include better access to basic financial services, the provision of low-cost accounts, notice provisions for branch closures, and a broadening of the existing Bank Act provision on coercive tied selling. Moreover, federal financial institutions with equity in excess of $1 billion will be required to provide annual public accountability statements that describe their contributions to the Canadian economy and society.

See also

- Banking in Canada
- Credit Union
- List of banks in Canada

External links

- Bank of Montreal [1]
- Bank of Nova Scotia [2]
- CIBC [3]
- National Bank of Canada [4]
- Royal Bank of Canada/RBC [5]
- TD Bank Financial Group [6]

Royal Bank of Canada

Type	public TSX: RY [1] NYSE: RY [2] SIX: RY [3]
Industry	financial services
Founded	Halifax, Nova Scotia, 1864
Headquarters	Montreal, Quebec, Canada Toronto, Ontario, Canada
Key people	Gordon Nixon, chief executive officer
Revenue	$29.1 billion CAD (2009)
Net income	▲ $3.9 billion CAD (2009)
Total assets	$655.0 billion CAD (2009)
Employees	71,186 (Full-time equivalent, 2009)
Website	rbc.com [4]

The **Royal Bank of Canada** (in French, **Banque Royale du Canada**, and commonly **RBC** in either language) is the largest financial institution in Canada, which is measured by deposits, revenues, and market capitalization. The bank serves seventeen million clients and has 80,100 employees worldwide. The company's primary corporate offices are located in Toronto, Ontario, while it is officially headquartered in Montreal, Quebec. The bank was founded in 1864 in Halifax, Nova Scotia. RBC's Institution Number (or bank number) is 003.

In Canada, the bank is branded as *RBC Royal Bank* in English and *RBC Banque Royale* in French and serves approximately ten million clients through its network of 1,197 branches. *RBC Bank* is the US retail banking subsidiary with 439 branches across six states in the Southeast, which serve more than a million customers. RBC also has 127 branches across seventeen countries in the Caribbean, which serve more than 1.6 million clients. RBC Capital Markets is RBC's worldwide investment and corporate banking subsidiary, while the investment brokerage firm is known as RBC Dominion Securities. Investment banking services are also provided through RBC Bank and the focus is on middle market clients.

RBC is listed as the largest Canadian company by revenue and market capitalization by The Globe and Mail and is ranked at number 53 on the Forbes Global 2000 listing. The company has operations in Canada, the United States, and 51 other countries.

Timeline

- 1864 - Merchants Bank founded in Halifax.
- 1869 - Changed name to Merchants' Bank of Halifax.
- 1869 - Federal charter received.
- 1870 - 1880s - Expansion in Maritime Provinces.
- 1901 - Changed name to Royal Bank of Canada (RBC).
- 1907 - Head Office moved from Halifax to Montreal.
- 1910 - Merged with Union Bank of Halifax.
- 1910 - bank at Carrère and Hastings, Winnipeg, Manitoba in 1910 in beaux-arts classicism proclaimes the financial dominance of Winnipeg in the prairies.
- 1912 - Merged with Toronto-based **Traders Bank of Canada** in order to improve its position in Ontario.
- 1917 - Merged with Quebec Bank, which was founded in 1818 and chartered in 1822 in Quebec City.
- 1918 - Merged with **Northern Crown Bank**, which was the result of the merger in 1908 between **Northern Bank** (established in 1905 in Winnipeg) and **Crown Bank of Canada** (1904), based in Ontario. RBC's acquisition gave it a strong presence in Manitoba and Saskatchewan.
- 1925 - Merged with **Union Bank of Canada**, which had begun in Quebec City in 1865 as the **Union Bank of Lower Canada**, but changed its name in 1886. Union Bank of Canada had moved its headquarters to Winnipeg in 1912, and built a strong presence in the Prairie Provinces.
- 1932 - RBC closed its branch in St. Lucia.
- 1959 - RBC opened a branch in St. Vincent.
- 1960 - RBC returned to St. Lucia.
- 1961 - Installed its first computer, which was the first in Canadian banking.
- 1964 - RBC opened a branch in George Town, Grand Cayman.
- 1993 - Merged with Royal Trust.
- 2000 - Merged merchant credit/debit card acquiring business with BMO Bank of Montreal's to form Moneris Solutions.
- 2000 - Acquired Dain Rauscher Wessels, a US brokerage and investment banking firm based in Minneapolis, Minnesota
- 2006 - Created Institutional Investment Joint Venture with Dexia. It is a 50/50 Partnership called RBC Dexia Investor Services. [5]

International timeline

RBC Royal Bank has carved out a name for itself as a leader in the Caribbean region, especially in the anglophone Caribbean.

The Royal Bank Plaza building in Toronto, Ontario

An RBC branch in Richmond Hill, Ontario.

- 1882 - Merchants Bank of Halifax opened an office in Bermuda.
- 1899 - RBC opened an agency in New York and a branch in Havana.
- 1903 - RBC bought **Banco de Oriente de Santiago de Cuba**. By the mid-1920s, RBC had 65 branches in Cuba and is the largest bank in the country.
- 1904 - RBC bought **Banco del Commercio de Havana**.
- 1907 - RBC opened a branch in San Juan, Puerto Rico; branches in Mayagüez and Ponce followed.
- 1909 - RBC established a branch in Nassau, Bahamas.
- 1910 - RBC opened a branch in London and acquired branches in Puerto Rico and Port of Spain, Trinidad as a result of its acquisition of Union Bank of Halifax.
- 1911 - RBC opened an agency in New York City, and branches in Bridgetown, Barbados, and Kingston, Jamaica.
- 1912 - RBC bought **Bank of British Honduras** (incorporated in 1902 by United States citizens from Mobile) in British Honduras, which it converted to a branch.

  RBC opened a branch in the Dominican Republic; three more follow.
- 1913 - RBC opened a branch in Grenada.
- 1914 - RBC bought out **Bank of British Guiana** (est. 1836), in British Guiana, and converted it to a branch.
- 1915 - RBC opened branches in Costa Rica, Antigua, Dominica, and St. Kitts.
- 1916 - RBC opened a branch in Venezuela.
- 1917 - RBC opened branches in Antigua, Dominica, St. Kitts, Montserrat, Nevis, and Tobago.
- 1918 - RBC opened a branch in Barcelona, and another in Vladivostok that lasted less than a year.

- 1919 - RBC opened branches in Brazil, Argentina, Uruguay, Paris, Martinique, Guadaloupe, and Port-au-Prince, Haiti.
- 1920 - RBC opened a branch in Colombia and a branch in Castries, St Lucia.
- 1923 - RBC bought and consolidated the banking operations of **Pedro Gomez Mena e Hijo** in Cuba.
- 1925 - RBC opened a branch in Peru, and acquired the American-owned, and failed, Bank of Central and South America. The purchase of BCSA brought with it subsidiaries, and their branches, in Colombia, Costa Rica, Peru, and Venezuela

Royal Bank branch

- 1940 - RBC closed its Branches in Martinique and Guadaloupe.
- 1960 - The Castro regime acquired the RBC's operations in Cuba. At the time of the forced sale, RBC had 24 branches in Cuba. From 1961 to 1965, RBC maintained a Special Representative in Havana to facilitate trade between Cuba and Canada. Actually, the Special Representative's primary function after the failed Bay of Pigs invasion in April 1961 was to act as a financial intermediary between the American and Cuban governments to manage the ransoming of the prisoners for food and agricultural machinery.
- 1970s - As a result of Law 75, RBC's operations in Colombia became **Banco Royal Colombiano**.
- 1973 - RBC was forced to incorporate its operations in Jamaica, which became Royal Bank (Jamaica).
- 1980 - RBC purchased Banco de San Juan in Puerto Rico, adding its 14 branches to the six that RBC already had in Puerto Rico. :RBC sold to Republic Bank of Trinidad and Tobago, its assets in Grenada.
- 1985 - RBC started to withdraw from much of the Caribbean.

  It sold its 12 branches in the Dominican Republic to Banco de Comercio Dominicano.

  It also sold its stake in Royal Bank (Jamaica) to Jamaica Mutual Life Assurance.

  The Government of Guyana nationalized its operations there and renamed the bank the National Bank of Industry and Commerce Ltd. [6], [7], [8]

  Additionally RBC incorporated its operations in Trinidad and Tobago locally, floating the shares, thereby divesting itself of ownership. The new bank took the name Royal Bank of Trinidad and Tobago (RBTT).
- 1986 - RBC sold its two branches in Haiti to Societe Generale Haitienne de Banque, a local bank.
- 1987 - RBC sold its operations in Belize, ex-British Honduras, to Belize Holdings Inc., which renames them Belize Bank.

- 1993 - RBC sold Royal Bank of Puerto Rico to Spain's Banco Bilbao-Vizcaya.
- 1995 - RBC sold Royal Trust Bank (Austria) to Anglo Irish Bank, which renamed it Anglo Irish Bank (Austria).
- 2001 - RBC acquired Centura bank based in Rocky Mount, North Carolina.
- 2003 - RBC purchased Florida interest in Provident Financial Group, Cincinnati OH
- 2006 - RBC upgraded its representative Office in Beijing, China to a branch.
- 2007 - RBC announced its acquisition of RBTT, after withdrawing from Trinidad and Tobago 20 years earlier.[9] [10]
- 2008 - RBC established a representative office in Mumbai, India. RBC re-acquired 98.14% of the shares of Royal Bank of Trinidad and Tobago.

RBC Bank (USA)

Main article: RBC Bank

A typical RBC Bank branch in Durham, North Carolina.

RBC has a large retail banking presence in the southeastern United States, marketing itself there as RBC Bank. RBC Bank is headquartered in Raleigh, North Carolina. The bank has recently merged with Flag Bank, increasing its presence in Georgia. RBC continues to grow in the Southeast after acquiring 39 branches of AmSouth Bank in Alabama on March 9, 2007 (previously RBC Centura had no locations in this state). RBC announced on January 17, 2008 that it would abandon the "Centura" brand in April 2008 and the U.S. operations would operate as RBC Bank. RBC's footprint in Alabama, Georgia, and Florida expanded significantly after it completed its acquisition of Alabama National BanCorporation in June 2008.

Scott Custer, Chairman and CEO of RBC's US Operations, retired on November 1, 2009.

Logo

The bank's symbol is a golden lion clutching a globe, on a blue background. An older version had a crown above the globe and had the lion facing to the left rather than the right. The change coincided with an expansion in United States markets. The logo is known and recognized in Canada as a famous symbol.[citation needed]

Corporate governance

Edson Loy Pease (1856–1930), a Quebec native, was a chief executive and managing director of the bank and one of the key people in its history. An employee of the Merchants' Bank of Halifax, he built that bank's Quebec business to where Montreal became its centre of operations. His efforts saw the Bank formally relocate its head office in 1907 to St. James Street in Montreal following which he induced the prominent Montreal business magnate Herbert S. Holt to accept an appointment as the bank's new President. While at the time Holt's presidency was largely a ceremonial position, his name substantially raised the bank's profile and broadened its business connections.

The title of Royal Bank's top executive has changed several times. Initially it was styled as *President*. Later, it became *Chief Executive Officer* and one often carried additional responsibilities as *Chairman of the Board*, while the second-in-command was the *President*. Allan R. Taylor was Chairman and CEO from 1986 to 1994, and he was succeeded by John Cleghorn in that capacity from 1994-2001. Gordon Nixon is currently the *President and Chief Executive Officer*, as the bank decided to appoint a non-executive chairman after Cleghorn's retirement.

Chief Executive

- Thomas Edward Kenny (1879–1908)
- Herbert Samuel Holt (1908–1934)
- Morris W. Wilson (1934–1946)
- Sydney Dobson (1946–1949)
- James Muir (1949–1960)
- W. Earle McLaughlin (1960–1979)
- Rowland C. Frazee (1977–1980)
- Jock K. Finlayson (1980–1983)
- Allan R. Taylor (1983–1986) - Chairman and CEO (1986–1994)
- John E. Cleghorn (1986–2001) - Chairman and CEO (1994–2001)
- Gordon Nixon (2001–present) - President and CEO (2001–present)

Chairman (non-executive)

- Guy Saint-Pierre (2001–2004)
- David P. O'Brien (2004–present)

Current members of the board of directors are: Geoff Beattie, Douglas Elix, John Ferguson, Paule Gauthier, Jacques Lamarre, Brandt Louie, Gordon Nixon, David O'Brien, Robert Peterson, Pedro Reinhard, Timothy Hearn, Kathleen P. Taylor, Victor Young, Michael McCain, Alice Labeige.

History of Head Offices

- 1976–present: Royal Bank Plaza, at 200 Bay Street, Toronto, Ontario.
- 1962-1976: Place Ville-Marie, at University Street & René-Lévesque Blvd, Montreal, Quebec.
- 1928-1962: "Old Royal Bank Building, Montreal", at 360 Saint Jacques Street, Montreal, Quebec.
- 1907-1928: Four Pillars Building (now destroyed), at 147 Saint Jacques Street, Montreal, Quebec.
- 1864-1907: Merchants' Bank of Halifax Building, on Bedford Row, Halifax, Nova Scotia.

RBC's official legal corporate headquarters still remains in Montreal at Place Ville-Marie. However, the great majority of management operations were moved to its current location in Toronto at the Royal Bank Plaza, making this the company's operational corporate headquarters.

Awards and recognition

RBC has been awarded with many awards and recognition for its financial products and services. RBC is the most "valuable brand" in Canada for over three consecutive years. RBC is also one of the top 100 sustainable companies in the world. Other awards and recognitions include:

- In 2007, awarded the "Best Bank" in Canada by *The Banker*, one of the oldest banking magazines,
- In 2007, RBC was recognized as the Top Most 100 powerful brands in the world,
- Was recognized as the "most respected corporation" in Canada
- In October 2008, RBC was named one of "Canada's Top 100 Employers" by Mediacorp Canada Inc., and was featured in *Maclean's* newsmagazine. Later that month, RBC was also named one of Greater Toronto's Top Employers, which was announced by the Toronto Star newspaper.

According to a global Newsweek ranking, which measures how effectively companies manage environmental risks and opportunities relative to their industry peers, Royal Bank of Canada is the most environmentally friendly company in the world.

RBC Blue Water Project

RBC has a longstanding commitment to environmental sustainability. Water has become an integral part of that commitment, as it is fundamental to the sustainability of all life on the planet. The RBC Blue Water Project is a 10-year, $50 million philanthropic commitment to support charitable organizations that are committed to watershed protection and providing access to clean drinking water.

More information about RBC Blue Water Project are available on the official webpage.

Sponsorship

In 2002, RBC purchased the naming rights for the Entertainment and Sports Arena in Raleigh, NC, home to the Carolina Hurricanes of the National Hockey League and North Carolina State University basketball. The arena was renamed the RBC Center, with a 20-year lease at a cost of $80 million. In June 2006, the RBC Center was host for the NHL's Stanley Cup Finals, and on June 19, 2006, the Carolina Hurricanes defeated the Edmonton Oilers in the RBC Center to win the Stanley Cup.

RBC sets aside one percent of its average annual net income before taxes for charitable partnerships via the arms-length RBC Foundation. They are also a major sponsor of numerous events such as the RBC Canadian Open and the Toronto International Film Festival, and are the longest-running Canadian sponsor of the Olympic Games. RBC was the co-presenting sponsor, along with Coca-Cola, of the 2010 Winter Olympics torch relay. They employ dozens of top-tier athletes as part-time spokespeople through the RBC Olympians program.

Controversies

On January 15, 2007, CBC Radio reported RBC is "refusing" people of certain nationalities to open U.S. dollar accounts with the bank. Canadian citizens with dual citizenship in Cuba, Iran, Iraq, Myanmar, North Korea or Sudan (mostly countries with U.S. sanctions) are affected. The U.S. Treasury Department restricts certain foreign nationals from using the U.S. dollar payment system to limit terrorism and money laundering after the September 11, 2001 attacks. RBC replied that compliance with such laws does not represent an endorsement by the bank and on January 17, clarified its position on the application of the U.S. laws, specifying that "with some exceptions" it does open accounts for dual citizens of the sanctioned countries. *Toronto Star* business and consumer affairs columnist Ellen Roseman regularly reported on RBC lack of customer service.

Certain environmental groups have criticized RBC's financing of oil sands bitumen extraction and expansion, cumulatively issuing "more than $2.3 billion in loans and financing more than $6.9 billion in [corporate] debt between 2003 and 2007 for 13 companies including: EnCana, Husky Energy, OPTI Canada, Delphi Energy, Canadian Oil Sands Trust, Northwest Upgrading, Suncor, Total, Connacher Oil and Gas, InterPipeline and Enbridge." The oil sands development has caused damage to the Athabasca River watershed and the people of the Cree Nation. The tailing ponds of water polluted by bitumen processing are extensive.

2010 Ottawa branch fire bombing

An RBC branch in The Glebe neighbourhood of Ottawa was firebombed in May 2010. The party responsible later identified themselves on Indymedia as opposed to the upcoming G20 meetings in Toronto as well as RBC's sponsorship of the 2010 Olympics in Vancouver.

Memberships

RBC is a member of the Canadian Bankers Association **(CBA)** and registered member with the Canada Deposit Insurance Corporation **(CDIC)**, a federal agency insuring deposits at all of Canada's chartered banks.
It is also a member of:

- CarIFS ATM Network
- Interac
- MasterCard in the Caribbean markets, and, beginning in March 2010, in Canada as well.
- NYCE point of sale Network
- Plus Network

References

- McDowall, Duncan. 1993. *Quick to the Frontier: Canada's Royal Bank.* Toronto: McClelland & Stewart, 1993 and (in French as) *Au coeur de l'action: Banque Royale*, Montreal: les Editions de l'Homme, 1993.

Canada China Business Council

External links

- Official Sites:
  - RBC [1]
  - RBC Bank [2] (USA)
  - RBC Dominion Securities [3]
  - RBC Royal Bank of Canada [4]
  - RBC Royal Bank of Canada (Caribbean and Bahamas) [5]
  - RBC Wealth Management, International [6]

Historical bank notes

- 1920 Trinidad and Tobago banknote (front) [7] - Example of Royal Bank Caribbean banknotes
- 1920 Trinidad and Tobago banknote (back) [8] - Example of Royal Bank Caribbean banknotes
- 1938 Saint Kitts banknote (front) [9] - Example of Royal Bank of Canada banknotes
- 1938 Saint Kitts banknote (back) [10] - Example of Royal Bank of Canada banknotes
- 1929's advertisement on a Chinese newspaper [11] - The Royal Bank of Canada advertisement on a Canada Chinese Newspaper, location coverpage bottom left, dated 10 May, 1929.

Toronto-Dominion Bank

Type	Public TSX: TD [1] NYSE: TD [2] TYO: 8640 [3]
Industry	Financial services
Founded	Toronto, Ontario, 1955 Bank of Toronto, 1855 Dominion Bank, 1869
Headquarters	Toronto, Ontario, Canada
Key people	W. Edmund Clark, chief executive officer
Revenue	$17.9 billion CAD (2009)
Net income	▲ $3.1 billion CAD (2009)
Total assets	$557.2 Billion CAD (2009)
Employees	65,930 (Full-time equivalent, 2009)
Subsidiaries	TD Canada Trust
Website	www.td.com [6]

The Toronto-Dominion Centre

The Toronto-Dominion Bank (in French, **Banque Toronto-Dominion**, and commonly **TD** in either language) is the second largest bank in Canada by market capitalization and deposits and the sixth largest bank in North America. The bank was created in 1955 through the merger of The Bank of Toronto and The Dominion Bank, which were founded in 1855 and 1869, respectively. TD's Institution Number (or bank number) is 004.

The bank operates as *TD Bank Financial Group* (in French, *Groupe Financier Banque TD*) and has over 74,000 employees and over seventeen million clients worldwide. In Canada, the bank operates as TD Canada Trust and serves more than 11 million customers at over 1,100 branches. In the

United States, the company operates as TD Bank (the initials are used officially for all U.S. operations). The current U.S. subsidiary was created through the merger of TD Banknorth and Commerce Bank, and serves more than 6.5 million customers with a network of more than 1,000 branches in the eastern United States.

The company is ranked at number 86 on the Forbes Global 2000 2010 listing. In October 2008, the company was named in the listings of Canada's Top 100 Employers in *Maclean's* and Greater Toronto's Top Employers by the *Toronto Star*.

TD Canada Trust Tower; one of the towers in downtown Toronto that houses the corporate offices of TDBFG

Operations

The bank's headquarters is at the Toronto-Dominion Centre at King Street and Bay Street in Toronto. The towering black skyscrapers were designed by the firm of Ludwig Mies van der Rohe and were the first of their kind in the city. Opened in 1967, the TD Centre was the inspiration of Al Lambert (1911–2002), the former President and Chairman of the Board of the bank.

TD Bank Financial Group subsidiaries include:

- TD Ameritrade - Online discount brokerage and wealth management (owns < 45%)
- TD Asset Management - Global asset management
- TD Bank, N.A. - official merger of bank charters for Commerce Bank or Commerce Bancorp, TD Banknorth and TD Bank USA on June 1, 2008
- TD Canada Trust - Canadian personal and commercial banking
- TD Commercial Banking - Global commercial banking
- TD Insurance - Insurance products and services, including a division that specializes in Alumni/Professional group rates (formerly Meloche Monnex)
- TD Securities - Global wholesale banking
- TD Waterhouse - Investment and wealth management
- Symcor Transaction processing outsourcing, e.g. cheques, bills and statements. (1/3 owned by each of the Royal Bank of Canada, the Bank of Montreal and the Toronto-Dominion Bank.)

Wealth Management offers investors an array of investment products and services. Wealth Management comprises a number of advisory, distribution and asset management businesses, including TD Ameritrade and TD Mutual Funds.

TD Securities is the investment banking arm of TD Bank Financial Group. It is an underwriter of debt and equity securities and strategic advisor to corporations, governments, and institutions worldwide. A key business segment is the trading of fixed income and equity products, currencies, commodities and derivatives in major financial markets around the world. It has offices in 18 cities worldwide with over 3,000 employees. TD Securities is a leading investment dealer in North America, has a strong presence in Europe, and is active in Asia.

History

The origins of The Toronto-Dominion Bank lie in the efforts of a group of Ontario businessmen involved in the buying, milling and marketing of grain. They were determined to create a financial institution to meet their specific needs in banking, insurance and commodities exchange. The first petition to the provincial legislature, in 1854, for the incorporation of The Millers, Merchants and Farmers Bank of Canada West, was rejected. However, on March 18, 1855, their application for a charter for The Bank of Toronto, with an authorized capital of £500,000, was granted.

In July 1856, the Bank of Toronto opened its offices at 78 Church Street, Toronto, with a staff of three and immediately began development of a provincial network of branches. In 1860, it opened its first branch outside of Ontario, in Montreal.

The Bank of Toronto established itself as an efficient, profitable, but essentially conservative bank through the 19th century. It maintained a very high reserve against its capital and enjoyed the highest share price of any bank in Canada. Growth was very slow and deliberate with a few new branches opened in emerging regional centres. Core customers remained farmers, merchants, and processors of farm products (millers, brewers, distillers).

In 1871, the Bank of Toronto was joined on the Ontario scene by the Dominion Bank, launched by entrepreneurs and professionals under the leadership of James Austin. They were dedicated to creating a new institution "conducive to the general prosperity of that section of the country." Like the Bank of Toronto, the Dominion Bank was a cautious institution, "selecting its customers carefully, serving them well, and duly prospering with them" (in the words of the official history). It too created a network of branches, and in 1872 became the first Canadian bank to have two branches in one city – Toronto.

With the maturing of the Canadian economy and the opening of northern Ontario and the West in 1880s and 1890s, the banks became more aggressive in loans to resource industries, utilities, and manufacturing. In 1897, the Dominion Bank opened its first western branch in Winnipeg and two years later the Bank of Toronto opened a branch in the British Columbia mining town of Rossland. In the first decade of the twentieth century, the banks rapidly expanded their branch networks in central Canada and across the west.

To mark their rise as significant national institutions, the Dominion Bank moved into a large new head office building at the corner of King and Yonge Streets in Toronto in 1879 and the Toronto Bank followed with another landmark head office at King and Bay Street in 1913.

World War I brought new challenges for the two banks when they were called upon to finance war expenditures and to support the innovation of war bonds marketed to the general public. Half the staff of the two banks served in the armed forces.

Except for some contraction in the western provinces due to drought, the decade following the war was one of expansion and increasing profitability due to resource development and industrial expansion. Both banks weathered the storm of depression in the 1930s without great difficulty, despite a decline in earnings. Like all Canadian banks, they endured criticism of its credit policies and resisted the introduction of a central bank to control the money supply and advise on fiscal policy. Ultimately the Bank of Canada was established and the banks relinquished their right to issue their own currency.

The coming of the Second World War involved the banks, once again, in the marketing of war bonds and in participation in the control of foreign exchange, rationing, and other financial war measures. Approximately 500 staff, or almost half the total, entered the armed forces.

The Bank of Toronto and Dominion Bank emerged from the war in 1945 stronger than ever, with assets more than doubled since 1939. With the post-war boom they became more active in business lending and in the penetration of new markets. However, they quickly realized that the costs of expansion and competition with much larger rivals made their objectives difficult to realize. Neither bank had engaged in acquisitions or mergers in order to grow, but both determined that a union with a bank of equal size would place them in a much stronger position to take advantage of the opportunities of the post-war economy.

In 1954 negotiations began between the Bank of Toronto and the Dominion Bank, and by the end of the year an amalgamation agreement was reached. In their brief to the Minister of Finance the banks stated: "It is more burdensome for a small bank to keep pace with the development of our country than for a large bank, with the result that the effective growth and comparative influence of smaller banks will probably in the future decline in comparison with that of the larger banks."

On November 1, 1954, Canada's minister of finance announced that the amalgamation was accepted and shareholders were asked for their approval. This was forthcoming in December and on February 1, 1955, the Bank of Toronto and The Dominion Bank became the Toronto-Dominion Bank.

The first years of the new bank were dedicated to the demands of amalgamating the two predecessors, institutions of roughly equal size, but with different strengths and unique corporate cultures. Head office functions were combined, branches were consolidated, and a new regional organization was established. An aggressive program of branch modernization and expansion extended TD's presence in its traditional markets and took it into new territory in the Maritime provinces and on the natural resource frontier. The identity of the new bank was established through an active public relations campaign focused on customer service - "The Best in Banking Service", the Bank's first slogan evolved into the highly successful "The Bank Where People Make the Difference".

The competitive banking environment, and the need for effective integration of two administrations, led the Bank to re-assess and modernize business practises and methods through the second half of the

1950s. Procedures were streamlined, new technology was introduced, and the human resource function acquired new importance as the Bank placed increased weight on customer service and product knowledge.

The Bank's emergence as a forward-looking institution was highlighted by the announcement in 1962 that it would have a new and very high profile head office in downtown Toronto. The Toronto-Dominion Centre, designed by Mies van der Rohe, the leading architect of the day, would include the tallest building in Canada. It would revolutionize both the skyline of Toronto and the public perception of TD.

By the 1960s, the Bank had solidified its domestic base and established its credentials as a major institution. It began to look beyond its traditional spheres of operation and to explore the international scene and opportunities, domestic and foreign, for large scale project financing. A network of U.S. representative offices was developed and partnerships with global merchant banks and venture capital operations were undertaken. Heralding a new commitment to independent and syndicated project financing, in 1967 the Bank undertook the financing of the massive Anvil lead-zinc-silver mining operation in the Yukon, the construction of the Rainbow crude oil pipeline in Alberta, and resource development ventures in Ireland.

The Bank Act of 1967 ushered in a period of enormous change on the Canadian financial scene. Banks were permitted for the first time to charge more than six-per-cent interest on loans, encouraging a new emphasis on personal and specialized consumer loans. More significantly, banks could now make mortgage loans on real estate and the mortgage loan portfolio quickly gained enormous significance.

By the close of 1960s the Bank's customer base had become more diverse and new products and services were being launched almost daily. The Visa card made its appearance (as Chargex) and mutual funds were marketed for the first time. In addition, the options for product and service delivery were greatly expanded thanks to computer and communications technology. An "On-Line Savings" system was introduced in Toronto in 1967 and ten years later the Green Machine appeared (the first "full-service" automatic teller machine (ATM)), greatly enhancing the customer service capabilities of the Bank.

To establish a modern and popular brand a new logo was introduced and an official "TD green" was adopted in 1969. In the same period, television and radio advertising were utilized for the first time in order to promote the new range of products.

The Bank kept in step with the times on other fronts as well. Women were encouraged to move into management roles and the first female bank manager was appointed in 1968. Little more than a decade later more than 40% of all management trainees were women.

International operations, which had gained in importance in the late 1960s, became a major focus of the Bank after 1970. New subsidiaries were launched in the United Kingdom, United States, and the Middle East. In 1970, TD became first Canadian bank to make a substantial investment in commercial banking in Hong Kong and by the end of the decade TD's role in international lending and money market trading was supported by operations in almost every corner of the globe.

Following upon the success of the Toronto TD Centre, the Bank was active in financing retail and commercial real estate projects across Canada. It was a partner in the Toronto Eaton Centre and participated in such major developments as the Pacific Centre in Vancouver, Edmonton Centre, TD Square in Calgary, and the Toronto-Dominion Bank Building in Halifax.

The Bank easily weathered the economic downturn of the early 1980s, showing consistent (and sometimes remarkable) revenue increases from 1980 to 1984. By the late 1980s, however, the Bank was caught up in the debt crisis in the developing world caused by the recession and the dramatic rise in interest rates. Significant loan losses were reported in 1987 and while the Bank participated actively in debt restructuring initiatives, it also committed itself to more conservative lending practices.

Despite the difficult economic conditions and the negative impact on earnings, the 1980s and early 1990s saw many positive developments. Deregulation began to break down the barriers between the various elements of the financial sector, particularly with the Bank Act of 1987. The Bank moved into the discount brokerage business in 1984 with the introduction of Green Line Investor Services and less than a decade later launched its full service brokerage, TD Evergreen. In 1987, Toronto Dominion Securities Inc. was established to provide corporate, treasury and investment banking services to corporate clients. In 1992 the Bank acquired the assets of a major trust company, Central Guaranty Trust and began the operation of TD Bank and Trust.

The 1990s saw TD responding swiftly to the challenges of the Internet and leading the way in e-banking. In 1996 the Bank's web site was created and TD Access: PC was launched, North America's first fully integrated banking and brokerage PC package. In 1998 Web Access was introduced and within a year e-banking services were available to a growing number of customers internationally. By the 21st century, the Bank had positioned itself as a multi-channel e-commerce company.

The need to build TD into a major player in world financial markets prompted the Bank to acquire Waterhouse Investor Services Inc. in 1996 (and in a stroke more than double its size as a discount broker). The $8 billion purchase of Canada Trust was completed in 1999 and the merger took effect in February 2000.

Canada Trust brought a history as long and as rich as that of the TD Bank itself. It had grown out of the same need for basic financial services in a young Canada. Local businessmen in London, Ontario, in 1864, founded it, as the Huron & Erie Loan and Savings Company. But through mergers it could trace an ancestry to 1855 and the establishment of the Canada Permanent Mortgage Corporation by many of the same individuals who established the Bank of Toronto. It also had direct ties to Toronto General Trusts, Canada's first trust company, incorporated in 1872. These institutions were instrumental in providing a pioneering farming community and residents of the growing towns across Canada with mortgage funds and other financial services.

Huron & Erie/Canada Trust established itself as a dynamic mortgage and trust company, first in Ontario, then across Canada through the late 19th and early 20th centuries. It was consistently aggressive in building its business and marketing its services and became an innovator in customer service. Following its merger with Canada Permanent in 1989, Canada Trust became the country's sixth largest financial institution.

The Canada Trust acquisition gave the Bank new momentum, significantly expanded the breadth and depth of the Bank's branch coverage, and enhanced TD's customer service commitment. Some have incorrectly referred to the new corporation as TD Canada Trust, though the latter only makes up the largest division. Toronto-Dominion Bank has now been operating under the brand **Toronto-Dominion Bank Financial Group** (TDBFG).

With the merger of Toronto-Dominion Bank and Canada Trust, the Competition Bureau required them to sell either their MasterCard or Visa business. Citibank Canada bought TD Canada Trust's MasterCard business and clients. TD began advertising their Visa cards under the corporate brand TD Visa.

In the 1990s, TD acquired US discount brokerage Waterhouse, renaming it "TD Waterhouse". In Canada, TD's own "Green Line" discount brokerage adopted the TD Waterhouse name.

In June 1999, TD spun off 42 million shares or 12.4 % of TD Waterhouse in an IPO, with shares priced at $35.28 CAD or $24 USD per share, earning $1.01 billion USD. In 2001, with the bursting of the Dot-com bubble and lower trade volumes that brought down Waterhouse's share price, TD bought back that minority stake at $9 USD per share for only $378 million USD, earning a tidy profit on the privatization. The acquisition was conditional on TD owning at least 90 percent of Waterhouse's outstanding common shares, and it owned almost 89 percent when the privatization was announced.

In 2003, TD held talks with E-Trade about merging TD Waterhouse with E-Trade, but they broke down over issues of control. On August 26, 2004, the Bank announced a definitive agreement to acquire a 51% interest in Banknorth Group, Inc. (now TD Banknorth), a bank in the US northeast. In 2005, TD announced an agreement to sell TD Waterhouse (USA) to Ameritrade; TD would own a 30% stake in the newly created TD Ameritrade.

In late September 2009 and early October 2009, significant technical problems related to the integration of computer systems with the previously purchased Commerce Bank caused chaos for many customers as funds for scheduled direct deposits were not available and account balances were reported incorrectly. The bank's telephone lines experienced extremely high call volume and branches were crowded with customers looking for information.

In April 2010, TD Bank acquired three failed banks in the United States. It acquired certain assets and liabilities of Riverside National Bank of Florida, First Federal Bank of North Florida and AmericanFirst Bank from the Federal Deposit Insurance Corporation (FDIC).

Mergers

- Bank of Toronto and The Dominion Bank 1955
- Central Guaranty Trust (acquisition of assets and branches) 1992
- Waterhouse Investor Services 1996
- Canada Trustco 2000
- Stafford Trading and Letco Trading 2002
- Laurentian Bank Retail Branches (Ontario-BC) 2003
- Banknorth NA 2005
- Commerce Bancorp 2007 (completed)
- Riverside National Bank of Fort Pierce, Florida 2010
- The South Financial Group Inc., (Operates in North & South Carolina as Carolina First and in Florida as Mercantile Bank) acquisition 2010

A former Commerce Bank in Tuckerton, New Jersey that was rebranded as TD Bank

Corporate governance

- W. Edmund Clark - President and CEO 2002–present
- John M. Thompson - Non-executive Chairman 2003–present
- Frank McKenna - Deputy Chairman

Current members of the board of directors of the company are: William Bennett, Hugh J. Bolton, John Bragg, W. Edmund Clark, Wendy Dobson, Donna Hayes, Henry Ketcham, Pierre Lessard, Brian M. Levitt, Harold MacKay, Irene R. Miller, Nadir H. Mohamed, Roger Phillips, Wilbur Prezzano, William Ryan, Helen Sinclair, Carole Taylor and John Thompson.

The title of Toronto-Dominion Bank's top executive has changed over the years. Initially it was styled as Chairman. Later, it became Chief Executive Officer and one often carried additional responsibilities as Chairman of the Board, while the second-in-command was the President. After the merger of the Toronto-Dominion Bank and Canada Trust, while Charles Baillie was Chairman and Chief Executive Officer of the combined entity, Clark was appointed President and Chief Operating Officer which solidified him as the eventual successor to Baillie. Upon Baillie's retirement, Clark became the President and Chief Executive Officer, as the bank decided to appoint John M. Thompson as non-executive chairman.

Past Presidents:

- A. C. Ashforth, 1955–1960
- Allen T. Lambert, 1960–1972
- Richard M. Thomson, 1972–1978
- Allan J. Boyle, 1978–1981
- Robert W. Korthals, 1981–1995

- A. Charles Baillie, 1995–2000

Past Chairmen

- B. S. Vanstone, 1955–1956
- A. C. Ashforth, 1956–1961
- Allen T. Lambert, 1961–1978
- Richard M. Thomson, 1978–1998
- A. Charles Baillie, 1998–2003

Past top executives:

- Herbert S. White, Executive Chairman (1960s-1970s)
- Allen T. Lambert (1960-1972), Chairman and President
- Richard M. Thomson (1972-1978), Chairman and CEO
- Robert W. Korthals (????-1995)
- A. Charles Baillie (1995-2002), Chairman and CEO
- W. Edmund Clark, President and COO (1947-2002)

Membership

TDBFG is a member of the Canadian Bankers Association (CBA) and registered member with the Canada Deposit Insurance Corporation (CDIC), a Government of Canada agency insuring deposits at all of Canada's chartered banks. It is also a member of:

- Interac
- NYCE ATM network
- Plus Network for VISA cards
- VISA International
- Cipf

Branch locations

Canada

- All provinces
- Northwest Territories
- Yukon Territory

United States

- Connecticut
- Delaware
- Florida
- Maine

- Maryland
- Massachusetts
- New Jersey
- New Hampshire
- New York
- North Carolina (fall 2010)
- Pennsylvania
- Rhode Island (fall 2010)
- South Carolina (fall 2010)
- Vermont
- Virginia
- Washington, DC

References

Bibliography

- Schull, Joseph, *100 years of banking in Canada : a history of the Toronto-Dominion Bank.* by Joseph Schull ; illustrated by Brad Smith. Vancouver : Copp Clark, c1958. ix, 222 p. : ill. ; 24 cm.

External links

Official Websites

- TD Asset Management [4]
- TD Ameritrade [5]
- TD Bank Financial Group [6]
- TD Ameritrade Holding Corporation [6]
- TD CanadaTrust [7]
- TD Capital [8]
- TD Commercial Banking [9]
- TD Bank, NA (Formerly Commerce Bank and TD Banknorth) [10]
- TD Insurance Home and Auto [11]
- TD Meloche Monnex [12]
- TD Securities [13]
- TD Waterhouse Canada [14]
- TD Financing Services [15]

TD stock profiles and quotes

- TD NYSE Stock Quote [16]
- TD TSX Stock Quote [17]
- Toronto-Dominion Bank stock performance chart [18] from GStock
- Yahoo! - The Toronto-Dominion Bank Company Profile [19]

Scotiabank

Type	Public TSX: BNS [1] NYSE: BNS [2] TTSE: SBTT [3]
Industry	Financial services
Founded	1832 Halifax, Nova Scotia
Headquarters	Toronto, Ontario (Executive head office) Halifax, Nova Scotia (Corporate head office)
Key people	**Richard E. Waugh** (CEO) Sabi S. Marwah (COO) Luc A. Vanneste (CFO)
Revenue	▲ $14.5 billion CAD (2009)
Net income	▲ $3.5 billion CAD (2009)
Total assets	▼ $496.5 billion CAD (2009)
Employees	67,802 (Full-time equivalent, 2009)
Website	scotiabank.com [4]

The **Bank of Nova Scotia** (in French, **Banque de Nouvelle-Écosse**, and commonly **Scotiabank** in English and **Banque Scotia** in French) is the third largest bank in Canada by deposits and market capitalization. The bank was founded in 1832 in Halifax, Nova Scotia, but has since moved its executive offices to Toronto, Ontario. Scotiabank has billed itself as "Canada's International Bank" due to its acquisitions primarily in Latin America and the Caribbean, but also in Europe and India as well.

The company ranks at number 92 on the Forbes Global 2000 listing and is currently under the leadership of Richard E. Waugh who serves both in the capacity of President and CEO.

Scotiabank has been active in the third quarter of 2010 purchasing two large Latin American units in Chile and Brazil from European banks in the United Kingdom and Germany, respectively.

History

Founded in Halifax, Nova Scotia in 1832, under the name of the Bank of Nova Scotia, to facilitate the trans-Atlantic trade of the time. The bank launched its branch banking system by opening in Windsor, Nova Scotia. The expansion was limited to the Maritime Provinces until 1882, when the bank moved west by opening a branch in Winnipeg, Manitoba. The Manitoba branch later closed but the experience of doing business in a grain-town encouraged the Bank to expand into the American Midwest, including Minneapolis in 1885 and Chicago in 1892.

Scotiabank also operates locations throughout Mexico, after the purchase of the Mexican bank Inverlat, and deals in all aspects of personal banking, business banking, and property and auto loans.

By 1900, The Bank of Nova Scotia had opened 38 branches across Canada, the United States and Jamaica. In Canada, the Bank was represented in all of the Maritime Provinces, Quebec, Ontario and Manitoba. In 1892, the Bank of Nova Scotia became the first Canadian bank to establish in Newfoundland – 55 years before the dominion joined Confederation.

Early international expansion

Scotiabank branch on Regent Street, Belize City, Belize

- 1885 - The bank opens its first branch outside Canada in Minneapolis.
- 1889 - The bank opens a branch in Kingston, Jamaica, the first branch of a Canadian bank outside Canada, the US, or the UK. By 1931 it has 12 branches in Jamaica.
- 1892 - The bank closes its branch in Minneapolis and transfers the business to the agency that it opens in Chicago, Illinois.
- 1899 - The bank opens a branch in Boston.
- 1906 - The bank opens a branch in Havana, Cuba. By 1931 it has three branches in Havana, and one branch each in Camaguey, Cienfuegos, Manzanillo, and Santiago de Cuba.
- 1907 - The bank opens an agency in New York.
- 1910 - The bank opens a branch in San Juan, Puerto Rico, and later another one in Fajardo.
- 1920 - The bank opens a branch in London, and another in Santo Domingo, Dominican Republic.
- 2010 - The bank arrives to Bogotá, Colombia.

In its early expansion the bank clearly followed trade and its customers' business - such as the trade of sugar, rum, and fish in Jamaica - rather than pursuing a strategy of expansion into international financial centres.

Scotiabank is a member of the Global ATM Alliance, a joint venture of several major international banks that allows customers of the banks to use their ATM card or check card at certain other banks within the Global ATM Alliance with no fees when traveling internationally. Other participating banks are Barclays (United Kingdom), Bank of America (United States), BNP Paribas (France), Deutsche Bank (Germany), and Westpac (Australia and New Zealand).

Mergers

The Bank has amalgamated with several other Canadian financial institutions through the years:

Bank	Year established	Year of amalgamation
Union Bank of PEI	1864	1883
Summerside Bank	1863	1901
Bank of New Brunswick	1820	1913
Metropolitan Bank of Canada	1902	1914
The Bank of Ottawa	1874	1919
Montreal Trust	1889	1994
National Trust	1898	1997
Inverlat (Mexico)	2002	2003
National Bank of Greece (Canada)	1969	2005
Banco Wiesse Sudameris (Peru)	1920	2007
Banco Sudamericano (Chile)	1991	2007

Many former branches of Montreal Trust and National Trust were rebranded "Scotiabank & Trust", and continue to operate as such.

Operating Units

Scotiabank has four divisions:

- **Canadian Banking** is the commercial banking division, offering savings and loan services. It includes 1009 branches , 2,750 ABMs, and 3 call centres. It offers telephone, wireless and Internet banking. Their brokerage unit is called the Wealth Management Group.

- **Scotia Capital Inc.** is the investment banking division, which helps large corporations, institutions, and governments obtain capital and credit. The Canadian investment banking division is known as **ScotiaMcLeod** and was formerly known as McLeod Young Weir Co. & Ltd., a company started by four young entrepreneurs: Donald Ivan McLeod, William Ewart Young, James Gordon Weir, and John Henry Ratcliffe. Metals trading is done under the name of **ScotiaMocatta**. **Scotia Waterous** is the well-regarded M&A division that operates exclusively within the oil & gas industry.
- **International Banking** is the merchant banking division, assisting its customers with international trade. Scotiabank's marketing material claims it is the leading provider of financial services in the Caribbean, and that it has the broadest Asian network of any Canadian bank.
- **e-Commerce/e-Banking at Scotiabank** manages wire transfers and payments.

As of 2009, Scotiabank services over 12.5 million customers and has over 500 billion dollars in assets. The bank employs over 69,000 employees all over the globe including: Europe, Asia, Latin America and the Caribbean. Scotiabank is Canada's most international bank with over 2000 branches in some 50 countries. As in the past, in 2009 some of the top management at Scotiabank announced a plan that it would once again play a part in general infrastructural development in the countries where it operates.

Corporate sponsorship and branding

Sports

- Scotiabank is now the title sponsor of Calgary's Scotiabank Saddledome as of 08 October 2010
- Scotiabank currently is the title sponsor for running events that are part of the Canada Running Series: Scotiabank Montreal 21k & 5k (April), Vancouver Half-Marathon & 5k Run/Walk (June) & Toronto Waterfront Marathon, Half-Marathon & 5k (September) and the Scotiabank Bluenose Marathon.
- As of October 2007, Scotiabank became a sponsor of CBC Television's *Hockey Night in Canada*, and the title sponsor of its Gemini award winning pregame show, *Scotiabank Hockey Tonight.*
- Scotiabank also is currently the Official Bank of the National Hockey League and National Hockey League Players' Association. And the official bank of the NHLPA, the NHL Alumni, the Canadian Women's Hockey League. Additionally, Scotiabank sponsors the Little NHL (native hockey league) and several girl's hockey festivals across Canada.
- Currently has the naming rights to the arena of the Ottawa Senators, branding it Scotiabank Place.
- Scotiabank can be seen as a primary sponsor for Champion Boxer Miguel Cotto during his 2009 bout with Manny Pacquio
- In 2006 Scotiabank was awarded the title as the official bank for the ICC's 2007 Cricket World Cup. During the event, several stadia and venues [5] across the Caribbean (and Guyana in South America) are to become outfited with Scotiabank automated banking machines.

- Since 2005, Scotiabank has been the title sponsor of the CFL playoffs semi-final and conference final games, with games titled as the Scotiabank East Semi-Finals and Scotiabank West Semi-Finals. This is in addition to being the official financial services provider to the Canadian Football League.
- Since 2008, Scotiabank has been the official team sponsor of Canadian Cricket Team and the title sponsor of National T20 Championship in Canada.
- In 2010, Scotiabank was a sponsor of the World Rally Championship's Corona Rally Mexico.

Culture

- In 2007, Scotiabank and Cineplex Entertainment partnered up to create a loyalty rewards program called *SCENE*. The program allows patrons to sign-up for a special card that grants them points which can be redeemed for free movies or concession discounts. Scotiabank customers can also request for a SCENE debit card which gives them points when used. A SCENE VISA card was also launched in early May. In addition, 5 Cineplex Entertainment locations were rebranded as "Scotiabank Theatres".
- For 2007 and 2008, Scotiabank has been the title sponsor of the Scotiabank Nuit Blanche event in Toronto. [6]
- Title sponsor, Scotiabank Giller Prize. [7]
- Scotiabank Hall of Brock University in St. Catharines, Ontario.
- Scotiabank Hall in the Marion McCain Arts and Social Sciences Building at Dalhousie University in Halifax, Nova Scotia

Recent events

- On November 6, 2006, two homemade bombs were placed within Scotiabank branches in Mexico City. One exploded, resulting in no deaths, while a second bomb was de-activated. Authorities were previously alerted to the presence of the bombs. A coalition of five leftist guerilla groups which support (but had no known connections to) protests in Oaxaca claimed responsibility.
- In December, 2006 Scotiabank announced it successfully acquired majority control of the fourth largest Jamaica-based Securities dealer Dehring Bunting & Golding Ltd. [8] (DB&G) ending weeks of speculation about the bid on the Jamaica Stock Exchange. The deal is expected to cost the Bank of Nova Scotia and it's Jamaican subsidiary between C$80 – $90 Million dollars to close the deal.
- On August 31, 2007 Scotiabank announced it has signed agreements to purchase 79 per cent of Banco del Desarrollo, Chile's seventh largest bank for US$810 million. These agreements are the first stage in a plan to purchase up to 100 per cent of Banco del Desarrollo. Scotiabank will be making a public share offering on the same terms and expects to acquire up to 100 per cent of Banco del Desarrollo, which would be valued at US$1.03 billion.

- In July 2008, E*TRADE sold its Canadian division to Scotiabank for CAN$444 million, as part of a program of selling off non-core assets. Scotiabank is investigating the expansion of the E*Trade service to their Caribbean markets as well.
- In October 2008 Scotiabank was considered one of the front-runners to buy Cleveland-based National City Corp. and re-enter the United States market, alongside Pittsburgh-based PNC Financial Services and Minneapolis-based U.S. Bancorp. Many local citizens in Cleveland considered Scotiabank as the best option, due to their longstanding absence from the U.S. market, which would've allowed most of National City's operations to stay in Cleveland. Scotiabank, however, backed out of the deal, and PNC would acquire National City with TARP funds on October 24, 2008 after National City became a victim of the subprime mortgage crisis.
- In 2010 a panel for the World Intellectual Property Organization (WIPO) ruled that Scotiabank as the sponsors of the Caribana festival, did not have grounds for being awarded the domain name caribana.com from its current owners Working Word Co-operative.
- Soon after Canadian regulators gave the go ahead for Canadian banks to begin mergers and acquisitions, Scotiabank announced it would takeover Commerzbank AG's Brazilian wholesale banking unit. This information was released on September 16th, 2010.
- Scotiabank announced on September 27th, 2010, that they would be purchasing Royal Bank of Scotland's Chilean wholesale banking unit worth around $900 million in assets.

Awards

- 2005 - "Bank of the Year" - For Mexico, the Caribbean and in Jamaica by LatinFinance .

Corporate governance

Current members of the board of directors of Scotiabank are: Ronald A. Brenneman, C.J. Chen, N. Ashleigh Everett, John Kerr, Michael Kirby, Laurent Lemaire, John T. Mayberry, Thomas O'Neill, Elizabeth Parr-Johnston, Alexis Rovzar de la Torre, Indira Samarasekera, Arthur Scace, Allan Shaw, Paul Sobey, Barbara Thomas, and Richard E. Waugh.

Former members of the board include: Peter Godsoe (former President and CEO of Scotiabank) and Cedric Ritchie (Former Chairman).

Unionization

Scotiabank has unionized relationships with employees in a number of locations around the world. In Canada, the sole unionized workplace is the domestic banking branch in Deep River, Ontario.

Membership

BNS is a member of the Canadian Bankers Association (**CBA**) and registered member with the Canada Deposit Insurance Corporation (**CDIC**), a federal agency insuring deposits at all of Canada's chartered banks. It is also a member of:

- Interac
- VISA International
- MasterCard in the Caribbean markets
- Plus Network for VISA card users
- NYCE ATM Network
- CarIFS ATM Network
- LINX network ATM network [9]
- MultiLink Network ATM network [10]
- MAGNA Rewards as part of the Scotiabank MAGNA MasterCard.
- Global ATM Alliance

Sources

Bank of Nova Scotia. 1932. *The Bank of Nova Scotia, 1831-1932*. Halifax: Bank of Nova Scotia.

The Scotiabank Story: A History of the Bank of Nova Scotia, 1832-1982. by Joseph Schull

See also

- List of banks in Canada
- Scotia
- Scottish-Canadian
- Scotia Plaza
- Scotiabank Place
- Scotia Place

External links

- Official website [4]

Bank of Montreal

Type	Public TSX: BMO [1] NYSE: BMO [2]
Industry	Financial services
Founded	1817 Montreal, Quebec
Headquarters	Montreal, Quebec, Canada Toronto, Ontario, Canada
Key people	**Bill A. Downe** (CEO) **David A. Galloway** (Chairman) Russel C. Robertson (CFO)
Revenue	$11.1 billion CAD (2009)
Net income	▲ $1.8 billion CAD (2009)
Total assets	$388.5 billion CAD (2009)
Employees	36,173 (Full-time equivalent, 2009)
Website	bmo.com [3]

The **Bank of Montreal** (in French, **Banque de Montréal**, commonly **BMO** in either language), or **BMO Financial Group**, is the fourth largest bank in Canada by deposits. The Bank of Montreal was founded in 1817 in Montreal, making it Canada's oldest bank. BMO's Institution Number (or bank number) is 001. In Canada, the bank operates as *BMO Bank of Montreal* and has more than 900 branches, serving over seven million customers. The company also has substantial operations in the Chicago area and elsewhere in the United States, where it operates as *Harris Bank* and as *BMO Harris*. BMO Capital Markets is BMO's investment and corporate banking division, while the wealth management division is branded as BMO Nesbitt Burns.

The company is ranked at number 189 on the Forbes Global 2000 list.

History

BMO (pronounced Bee-Moe) today is a major international bank with a large amount of connections across Canada and around the world. In 1977, BMO's operational headquarters moved to the First Canadian Place in Toronto, while its legal head office remained in Montreal. Today, Bank of Montreal has assets of more than $387 billion CAD. (Source: http://www.bmo.com)

Like the other Canadian chartered banks, it issued its own paper money. The bank issued notes 1817-1942. The end dates are the final dates appearing on notes, which may have circulated for some time after. The Bank of Canada was established through the Bank of Canada Act of 1934 and the banks relinquished their right to issue their own currency.

Architecture

The Bank of Montreal in Waterloo, Ontario formerly known as the Molson's Bank, built in 1914 is on the Registry of one of the Historical Places of Canada. The "Old Bank of Montreal" on 100 Victoria Street East, also known as the "Heritage Court", Amherst, Nova Scotia built in 1906 is on the Registry of Historical Places of Canada. The Bank of Montreal in Winnipeg, Manitoba, constructed in 1927, is on the Registry of Historical Places of Canada. The Bank of Montreal in Hamilton, Ontario built in 1928, is on the Registry of Historical Places of Canada. The Bank of Montreal in Corner Brook, Newfoundland and Labrador built in 1915 is on the Registry of Historical Places of Canada. The Bank of Montreal in Delta, British Columbia built in 1919 is on the Registry of Historical Places of Canada. The Bank of Montreal in New Westminster, British Columbia built in 1947 to 1948 is on the Registry of Historical Places of Canada. The Bank of Montreal in Ottawa, Ontario built in 1930 to 1932 is on the Registry of Historical Places of Canada. The Bank of Montreal constructed a 3-storey bank in 1818 on rue St-Jacques in Montreal. It was modelled after a Georgian townhouse with a small porch with a classical pediment supported by Doric columns.

Gallery

First Canadian Place, Canada's tallest building

Bank of Montreal on 3rd Avenue W Prince Rupert, British Columbia

Bank of Montreal building with horse and carriage

Bank of Montreal

Bank of Montreal

Bank of Montreal

Mergers

During its history, Bank of Montreal has merged with or acquired several other Canadian banks:

- Commercial Bank of Canada (1868)
- Exchange Bank of Yarmouth (1903)
- People's Bank of Halifax (1905)
- People's Bank of New Brunswick (1907)

BMO, Edmonton

- Bank of British North America (1918)
- Merchants Bank of Canada (1922), as well as several investment banking firms.
- Molson Bank (1925)
- Royal Bank of Canada (2000) - Merged merchant credit/debit card acquiring business with BMO Bank of Montreal's to form Moneris Solutions.

Executives

Founders

The following merchants signed the Articles of Association for the creation of the "Montreal Bank" on June 23, 1817:

1. Robert Armour (1781–1857) businessman, militia officer, and office holder
2. John C. Bush (? - 1859)
3. Austin Cuvillier (1779–1849)
4. George Garden (c.1772-1828), director from 1817 to 1826 and vice-president from 1818 to 1822.
5. Horatio Gates (1777–1834), merchant and banker, President of BMO 1832-1834
6. James Leslie (1786–1873); bank director
7. George Moffatt (1787–1865); bank director
8. John Richardson (c. 1754 - 1831)
9. Thomas A. Turner (1775 ? - 1834)

Presidents

1. John Gray (1817 to 1820); co-founder and first President
2. Samuel Gerrard (1820 to 1826)
3. Horatio Gates (1826); co-founder and President
4. John Molson (1826 to 1834)
5. Peter McGill (1834 to 1860)
6. Thomas Brown Anderson (1860 to 1869)
7. Edwin Henry King (1869 to 1873)
8. David Torrance (1873 to 1876)
9. George Stephen (1876 to 1881)
10. C. F. Smithers (1881 to 1887)
11. Donald Smith (1887 to 1905)
12. George Alexander Drummond (1905 to 1910)
13. Richard B. Angus (1910 to 1913)
14. Sir Vincent Meredith (1913 to 1927)
15. Sir Charles Blair Gordon (1927 to 1939)

16. Huntly Redpath Drummond (1939 to 1942)
17. George Wilbur Spinney (1942 to 1948)
18. B. C. Gardner (1948 to 1952)
19. Gordon Ball (1952 to 1959)
20. G. Arnold Hart, president from 1959 to 1967 and CEO from 1959 to 1974
21. Fred McNeil, CEO from 1975 to 1979
22. William D. Mulholland, CEO from 1979 to 1989
23. Matthew W. Barrett (1987 to 1990)
24. F. Anthony Comper (1990 to 2007)
25. Bill Downe (from March 1, 2007)

President was for a long time the highest-ranking title in the bank's history, however this was superseded by *Chief Executive Officer* in the modern era, starting with G. Arnold Hart. Several of his successors as President were CEO as well, however Matthew W. Barrett was the first top executive not to be styled president.

Chief Executive Officer

In the modern era, the senior officer of Bank of Montreal has been styled *President and Chief Executive Officer* beginning with G. Arnold Hart. That officer often also held the title *Chairman of the Board*, until 2003 when a non-executive chairman was appointed.

The title of the second-ranking executive has changed several times and has often been left vacant. For instance, F. Anthony Comper as the top deputy to Barrett was President and *Chief Operating Officer* from 1990 to 1999, until he became Chairman and CEO while retaining his title of President. During most of Comper's tenure as CEO, while there was no official "number two" executive, the CEO of BMO Capital Markets (the investment banking division) was largely considered the second-most powerful officer. Bill Downe ascended from CEO of BMO Capital to *Chief Operating Officer* of the entire group, but held the title only for a transitional period lasting a year until he succeeded Comper as President and CEO in 2007.

(partial list)

- Matthew W. Barrett (1990 to 1999)
- F. Anthony Comper (1999 to 2007)
- Bill Downe (from March 1, 2007)

Operations

BMO is divided into three "client groups" which serve different markets. Each of the client groups operates under multiple brand names.

- **Personal and Commercial Client Group** (retail banking), including
  - *BMO Bank of Montreal* (retail banking in Canada), including BMO's *Mosaik Mastercard* credit cards; *BMO Life*, a life insurance company; and the former virtual bank division mbanx
  - Harris Bank (retail banking in the United States, headquartered in Chicago)
- **Investment Banking Group** (known as *BMO Capital Markets*)
- **Private Client Group** (wealth management), including
  - *BMO Nesbitt Burns* (full service investing in Canada)
  - *BMO InvestorLine* (self-service investing in Canada)
  - *Harris Investor Services* (advisory services in the United States)
  - *BMO Harris Private Banking*

In October 2008, BMO Financial Group was named one of Greater Toronto's Top Employers by Mediacorp Canada Inc., which was announced by the Toronto Star newspaper.

Corporate governance

Current members of the board of directors of BMO are: Robert Astley, Stephen Bachand, David Beatty, Robert Chevrier, Bill Downe, Ronald Farmer, David A. Galloway, Harold Kvisle, Eva L. Kwok, Bruce Mitchell, Philip Orsino, Robert Prichard, Jeremy Reitman, Guylaine Saucier, Don M. Wilson III, and Nancy Southern.

Headquarters

BMO maintains its official legal corporate head office in Montreal, located on Saint-Jacques Street. However, the Chairman and President and most senior division executives work out of Toronto headquarters at First Canadian Place. Under the direction of the Toronto executive, the Montreal Place d'Armes office oversees the bank's economic (and, to some extent, political) relation with the province of Quebec. This reflects the preponderant place of the Toronto Stock Exchange and Bay Street in the Canadian economy.

Bank of Montreal's main Montreal branch at Place d'Armes in Montreal.

Sport events sponsorship

BMO is the sponsor for this season of the Toronto Maple Leafs, Toronto FC and the Toronto Raptors.

BMO Bank of Montreal is the current title sponsor for the marathon race for the Vancouver International Marathon Society held each year in May. The current name is "BMO Bank of Montreal Vancouver Marathon".

Bank of Montreal is also a major sponsor of Skate Canada, and is the title sponsor of the BMO Financial Group Canadian Championships, BMO Financial Group Skate Canada Junior Nationals, BMO Financial Group Skate Canada Challenges, BMO Financial Group Skate Canada Sectionals, and BMO Financial Group Skate Canada Synchronized Championships. It is also the presenting sponsor of the CanSkate Learn-to-Skate Program.[4]

BMO purchased the naming rights to the national soccer stadium (BMO Field) at Exhibition Place in Toronto, the home of the Major League Soccer team Toronto FC, which BMO is also sponsoring. BMO's logo is on the front of their jersey.

On July 23, 2008 it was announced that BMO signed a one-race deal with IndyCar team Newman/Haas/Lanigan Racing to appear on the #06 car of Graham Rahal in the first-ever IRL-sanctioned Canadian IndyCar race at Edmonton.

Recent mergers and merger attempts

Purchase of Harris Bankcorp (1984)

In 1984 the bank greatly expanded its operations in the United States by purchasing Chicago's Harris Bank.

Proposed merger with RBC (1998)

In 1998 Bank of Montreal shocked the Canadian financial community by announcing plans to merge with RBC. The Canadian government later blocked the proposed merger. In December 2000, the banks were successful in merging their credit and debit card processing services to form Moneris Solutions.

Purchase of GKST Inc (2008)

In 2008 Bank of Montreal bought Griffin, Kubik, Stephans, and Thompson. GKST was a Chicago based employer that employs about 100 people in sales, trading, research, public finance and underwriting, and specializes in municipal bonds, U.S. Treasury and agency debt, and mortgage-backed securities.

Purchase of AIG Life Insurance Company of Canada (2009)

In 2009, the Bank purchased AIG's Canadian life insurance business, AIG Life Insurance Company of Canada, for approximately $330 million CAD. The transaction, including 400,000 customers and 300 employees, makes BMO the second-biggest life insurer among Canadian banks. The company was renamed BMO Life Assurance Company.

Purchase of Diners Club International Franchise (2009)

In November 2009, Bank of Montreal announced the purchase of Diners Club International's North American franchise from Citibank. The transaction will give BMO exclusive rights to issue Diners cards in the U.S. and Canada. The deal closed in December 2009.

Membership

BMO is a member of the Canadian Bankers Association (CBA) and registered member with the Canada Deposit Insurance Corporation (CDIC), a federal agency insuring deposits at all of Canada's chartered banks. It is also a member of:

- Interac
- MasterCard International
- Cirrus Network for MasterCard card users
- Air Miles

References

- Denison, Merrill, 1893–1975. *Canada's first bank : a history of the Bank of Montreal.* Toronto: McClelland and Stewart, c1966. 2 v. : ill., maps, ports., (some folded, some col). ; 25 cm.
- Nolin-Raynauld, Michelle, 1926–. *The Bank of Montreal building on Place d'Armes, 1845–1901 /* Michelle Nolin-Raynauld ; foreword by Jean Bélisle ; translated by Judith Berman. Montreal : Varia Press, c1999. 143 p. : facsm., ill., plans ; 23 cm. Originally presented as the author's thesis (master—Université de Montréal), 1984, under the title: L'architecture de la Banque de Montréal à la Place d'Armes. Translation of: L'édifice de la Banque de Montréal à la Place d'Armes, 1845–1901. ISBN 2922245128
- BMO Financial Group Corporate Archives, Montreal
- Rupert *Canadian Investment Bank Review* McGraw-Hill Ryerson, Limited 1992

External links

Official sites

- BMO Bank of Montreal's web site [1]
- BMO Bank of Montreal's Rewards site [2]
- BMO 2008 Annual Report [3]

Other sites

- BMO stock quote [4] from TSX

Canadian Imperial Bank of Commerce

Type	Public TSX: CM [1], NYSE: CM [2]
Industry	Financial services, Banking
Founded	1867
Headquarters	Toronto, Ontario, Canada
Key people	Gerald T. McCaughey, CEO
Revenue	$9.9 billion CAD (2009)
Net income	▲ $1.2 billion CAD (2009)
Total assets	$335.9 billion CAD (2009)
Employees	41,941 (Full-time equivalent, 2009)
Subsidiaries	CIBC World Markets CIBC Retail Markets CIBC Imperial Service CIBC Wood Gundy
Website	www.cibc.com [3]

The **Canadian Imperial Bank of Commerce** (in French, **Banque Canadienne Impériale de Commerce**, and commonly **CIBC** in either language) is one of Canada's chartered banks, fifth largest by deposits. The bank is headquartered at Commerce Court in Toronto, Ontario. CIBC's Institution Number (or bank number) is 010.

CIBC also operates in the United States, the Caribbean, Asia and the United Kingdom, and serves more than eleven million clients and has more than 40,000 employees worldwide. The company ranks at number 170 on the Forbes Global 2000 listing.

History

The Canadian Imperial Bank of Commerce, as it is known today, came into being in 1961. The bank was formed through the merger of the Canadian Bank of Commerce and the Imperial Bank of Canada. At the time, they were two of Canada's largest banks.

Canadian Bank of Commerce and Imperial Bank of Canada

Main articles: Canadian Bank of Commerce and Imperial Bank of Canada

The Canadian Bank of Commerce opened for business on May 15, 1867 in Toronto and was founded by The Honourable William McMaster as competition for the Bank of Montreal. It opened for business on May 15, 1867 in Toronto. By 1874 it had 24 branches.

The Imperial Bank of Canada opened in Toronto on March 18, 1875, founded by former Commerce Vice-president Henry Stark Howland.

By the end of 1895, The Canadian Bank of Commerce had 58 branches and the Imperial Bank of Canada 18.

Following the 1896 discovery of gold in the Yukon, the Dominion Government asked The Canadian Bank of Commerce to open a branch Dawson City. With acquisitions in the 1920s, The Commerce became one of the strongest branch networks in Canada with well over 700 branches. Internationally the bank opened branches in Cuba, Jamaica, Barbados and Trinidad during the 1920s.

Wood, Gundy & Company, the precursor of CIBC's investment banking arm, opened its doors on February 1, 1905. During World War I, they took a prominent and active role in the organization of Victory Loans.

1931-1960

The Canadian Bank of Commerce opened its new head office in Toronto in 1931. An observation gallery on the 32nd floor was a popular tourist attraction where, for the first time, visitors could get an aerial view of the city.

Commerce Building circa 1930 now known as Commerce Court North in Toronto.

In 1936, The Commerce was the first Canadian bank to establish a personal loans department.

Following the war, both banks started to open new branches. Although the banks had been barred from the mortgage business since 1871, the Canadian government now called upon them to provide mortgage services. So, in 1954, Canadian banks started offering mortgages for new construction.

In 1960, Imperial Chairman Stuart Mackersy approached Neil McKinnon the President of The Commerce with a proposal to merge the two banks. This followed a decade of expansion in the Canadian economy and Canada's capitalization of the industrialization of its natural resources. A deal between the two banks was quickly reached.

Creating the Canadian Imperial Bank of Commerce

On June 1, 1961, the Canadian Imperial Bank of Commerce was formed through the merger of The Canadian Bank of Commerce and the Imperial Bank of Canada which had over 1,200 branches across Canada. The new bank had the most resources and the most branches of any bank in the country.

Following the merger, the new bank needed a new head office. While planning to retain Commerce Court North, the bank hired architect I. M. Pei to design a 3-building complex. The result was Commerce Court consisting of a landscaped courtyard complementing the existing building and included the newly built 786-foot Commerce Court West. When it was completed in 1973, the 57-storey building was the tallest building in Canada, as well as the largest stainless-steel-clad building in the world.

Commerce Court in Toronto.

In 1967, both Canada and CIBC celebrated their centenaries. CIBC was the only chartered bank to have a branch on-site at Expo 67. It was also at this time that computerization began to change banking services. That same year the Yonge and Bloor branch in Toronto was the first Canadian bank branch to update customer bank books through computer. This also marked the introduction of inter-branch banking. Before the decade was out, CIBC had introduced the first 24-hour cash dispenser, which would eventually become the ATM.

1981-1998

Changes to federal and provincial regulations ending the separation of banks, investment dealers, trust companies and insurance companies came in 1987. CIBC quickly took advantage of this and became the first Canadian bank to operate an investment dealer, CIBC Securities, offering services to the public.

In 1988, CIBC acquired a majority interest in Wood Gundy Inc. who brought their reputation in underwriting as well as their name. Shortly thereafter Wood Gundy and CIBC Securities merged to become CIBC Wood Gundy which would later become CIBC Oppenheimer in 1997 and then CIBC World Markets.

In 1992, CIBC introduced automated telephone banking; in 1995 they launched their website, and shortly thereafter began offering banking services online. In 1998, CIBC joined with Loblaws to create President's Choice Financial which launched in 28 Ottawa area stores.

1998-present

There was an attempt by CIBC to merge with the Toronto-Dominion Bank in 1998. However, the Government of Canada at the lead of then Finance Minister Paul Martin blocked the merger from occurring.

CIBC sold their corporate and purchasing credit card business to US Bank Canada in October 2006. The buyer has previously acquired business charge cards from RBC.

In 2006, the stock ticker symbol on the New York Stock Exchange was changed from *BCM* to *CM* to bring it in line with the ticker symbol on the Toronto Stock Exchange.

In December 2006, CIBC acquired majority control of their publicly held joint venture FirstCaribbean International Bank for just over US$1billion (Bds$2 billion), from Barclays Bank 's acquiring their 43.7% stake.

On February 12, 2009 the Trinidad and Tobago Express newspaper reported that CIBC may enter into discussions to buy out CL Financial's stake in the Republic Bank of Trinidad and Tobago. Due to CL Financial financial issues during the Global financial crisis of 2008–2009. As of May 2010, no further information was available.

In February, 2010 CIBC became the first chartered bank in Canada to launch a Mobile Banking iPhone App. It surpassed 100,000 downloads in just over one month following launch, with over 1 million client logins to CIBC Mobile Banking since its introduction.

Mergers

Canadian Bank of Commerce

Halifax Banking Company - 1903 Established in 1825 by Enos Collins with Hon. Henry H Cogswell as President from 1825-1834:

- Robie Uniacke - President 1882-1903
- Horatio Newelham Wallace - Cashier 1892-1903

Gore Bank Formed in 1836 and merged with the Commerce in 1870:

- Colonel James W Wythe - President 1836-1839
- Colin C Ferrie - President 1839-1856
- Andrew Steven - President 1856-1861; Cashier 1836-1856
- Thomas Clark Street - President 1862-1868; later Bank of Commerce Director

Eastern Townships Bank Formed in 1859 and merged with the Commerce in 1912:

- Colonel Benjamin Pomroy - President 1859-1874
- Richard W Heneker - President 1874-1902
- William Farnell - President 1902-1912

- James MacKinnon - Cashier 1902-1912

Bank of British Columbia Established with a Royal Charter in 1862 and merged with the Commerce in 1901:

- Thomas W.L. Mackean - Chairman 1862-1876
- Sir Robert Gillespie - Chairman 1876-1901
- Eden Colville - Director 1876-1893
- James Anderson - 1862-1897, Manager 1862, General Manager 1867-1875, Director 1876-1890

Merchants Bank of Prince Edward Island Formed 1856 and merged with the Commerce in 1906:

- W.A. Weekes 1864-1865
- Robert Longsworth 1871-1882
- Right Hon. Sir Louis Davies 1887-1897
- Benjamin Heartz 1897-1904
- W.A. Weekes 1904-1906

Bank of Hamilton merged with the Commerce in 1924.

The Standard Bank of Canada, which had begun as the St Lawrence Bank (1872–1876), merged with the Commerce in 1928.

Imperial Bank of Canada

- Niagara District Bank 1875
- Weyburn Security Bank 1931
- Barclays Bank (Canada) 1956

CIBC 1961

- Canadian Bank of Commerce 1867-1961
- Imperial Bank of Canada 1875-1961
- **Wood Gundy Incorporated 1988** - forming CIBC Wood Gundy and renamed CIBC World Markets.
- **TAL Private Management** 1994-2005 - formerly Timmins and Associates Ltd, merged with CIBC Investment Management Corporation in 1994, named changed to **TAL Global Asset Management Incorporated** in 1998 and finally full acquired by CIBC in 2001. Rename to **CIBC Asset Management** effective January 1, 2006.

CIBC-TD Bank

There was an attempt by CIBC to merge with the Toronto-Dominion Bank in the late 1990s. However, the Government of Canada at the lead of then Finance Minister Paul Martin blocked the merger from occurring.

CIBC in the Caribbean

In 1920, Canadian Bank of Commerce established its first branches in the West Indies in Bridgetown, Barbados and in Kingston, Jamaica. That same year it also opened branches in Port of Spain, Trinidad and Havana, Cuba. The bank had already opened a branch in Mexico City in 1910. In 1957, the bank opened a branch in Nassau, the Bahamas, and in the subsequent years expanded its operations in Jamaica. Between 1963 and 1988, the bank expanded its branch network in Barbados opened branches in St. Vincent, Antigua, and St Lucia. In 1988, CIBC sold 45% of its shares in CIBC Jamaica via a public share issue. Between 1993 and 1996, CIBC restructured its holdings in the Caribbean, with the incorporation of CIBC West Indies Holdings Limited and CIBC Caribbean Limited. CIBC West Indies Holdings then sold 30% of its shares to the public. In 1997, CIBC issued 5 million shares in CIBC Bahamas Limited to the public. On October 31, 2001 Barclays Bank PLC and CIBC agreed to combine their Caribbean operations to establish **FirstCaribbean International Bank**. In 2006, CIBC bought out Barclays Bank's stake to give it about 92% of FirstCaribbean International Bank. In 2010, CIBC acquired a 22.5% equity of Butterfield Bank of Bermuda.

Joint Ventures

- CIBC Mellon Global Securities Services: formed by CIBC and Mellon Bank Corp. (now Bank of New York Mellon) of Pittsburgh PA 1996 and Canada Trust's (now TD Canada Trust) pension and custody business in 1997
- Canadian Eastern Finance Limited (CEF): formed by CIBC and Hutchison Whampoa of Hong Kong; includes CEF Capital Limited, CEF Investment Management Limited
- President's Choice Financial: A joint venture between CIBC and Loblaw Companies Limited; PC Financial's banking services such as deposit accounts, investments and credit products (excluding Mastercard) are provided by a division of CIBC Retail Markets, formerly Amicus Bank. In 2005 Amicus was dissolved as a separate legal entity.
  - Amicus FSB: A similar setup as President's Choice Financial, it was created in 1999 in the United States with Winn Dixie and Safeway Inc. under the Marketplace Bank and Safeway Select Bank brands. It was disbanded in 2002 and sold to E*Trade Bank.
- Soltrus Inc 2001: provider of digital trust services for businesses and consumers to communicate and transact over digital networks owned by CIBC, Telus Corp and VeriSign Inc.
- Aplettix Inc 2000: firm specializing in secure transaction systems in the banking sector; CIBC signed an agreement with the New York based firm in 2000, but the project was later abandoned for

alternatives such as VeriSign
- Canadian Defence Community Banking - CIBC and the Department of National Defence have worked together to develop Canadian Defence Community Banking, a banking program created specifically to meet the unique needs of the Canadian military community. Services are provided by CIBC Retail Markets in the same way as the CIBC PC Financial products.

Restructuring and Outsourcing

- **EDULINX Canada Corporation**: Established in 1999, it was sold to Nelnet Canada Inc, the Canadian unit of Nelnet, Inc. of the U.S., in late 2004
- HP Intria Items (**Intria Corp**): Formed by CIBC with Hewlett Packard and Fiserv Canada in 1996. In 2005, CIBC acquired the remaining shares from Fiserv and Intria becomes a unit of CIBC
- **Toronto Blue Jays Baseball Club**: Founding owners of the MLB team in 1977 and had a 10% stake with majority owner Labatt's Breweries (later acquired by InterBrew NV) and sold to Rogers Media in 2000
- **TSYS** In 2002 a 10 year agreement was signed with **Total Systems Services Inc** of Columbus GA to outsource credit card processing operations
- **CIBC Leadership Centre**: In 2001, the King City facility was sold to **Benchmark Hospitality** as the bank began to divest real estate or investment in areas outside of its business strategies
- **Juniper Financial Corporation**: The bank acquired the Wilmington DE credit card issuer 2001 and sold to Barclays Bank in 2004

Current operations

Through its two major operating groups, CIBC Retail Markets and Wholesale Banking, CIBC provides a full range of financial service products and services to almost 11 million clients in Canada and around the world.

Company divisions

CIBC has two strategic business units:

- CIBC Retail Markets
- CIBC Wholesale Banking

The functional groups that provide support across CIBC are:

- Administration - comprises Human Resources, Legal, Corporate Security, Compliance, Control Division, Internal Audit, Corporate Secretary, Ombusdman, Privacy, and Communications and Public Affairs within CIBC.
- Corporate Development - is a key participant in creating long-term value for CIBC and its shareholders and in directing CIBC's strategic planning process.

- Finance - provides financial services to CIBC's businesses through effective governance and decision support processes.
- Risk Management - defines CIBC's risk appetite and sets risk strategy to manage risk in alignment with risk appetite and business strategy; measures, monitors and controls CIBC's exposure to risk; and oversees the allocation of risk resources.
- Technology and Operations - manages and enhances the technology and operational processes that run CIBC's businesses worldwide, as well as providing specialized service and advice to business partners.

Operational facts

- Total Employees (worldwide): 41,941 (2009)
- Total Branches (Canada): 1,069 (2009)
- Total ATMs (Canada): 3,850 (2009)
- Total Assets: $335.9 billion (2009)
- Market capitalization: $23.8 billion (2009)
- Revenue: $9.9 billion (2009)
- Net income: $1.2 billion or $2.65 per share (2009)
- In 2009, almost $27 million was contributed through the CIBC group of companies to charitable and non-profit initiatives in Canada. Of this, close to $20 million was for charitable donations, supporting a wide variety of national, regional and local organizations.

Memberships

CIBC is a member of the Canadian Bankers Association **(CBA)** and registered member with the Canada Deposit Insurance Corporation **(CDIC)**, a federal agency insuring deposits at all of Canada's chartered banks. It is also a member of:

- Interac
- VISA International Network
- Aeroplan Rewards
- Plus Network for VISA and bank cards

Corporate governance

CIBC is well known for its publicized battles of succession to the top position of President and CEO (formerly styled Chairman and CEO until 2003 when the positions were separated). When Al Flood became CEO, one of his first acts was to fire his chief rival Paul Cantor. 1999 saw a competition between Wood Gundy (now CIBC World Markets) chief John S. Hunkin and Personal/Commercial banking head Holger Kluge, with Kluge retiring the firm after Hunkin was selected. In February 2004,

Hunkin forced his friend and heir-apparent David Kassie to resign as Chairman and CEO of World Markets after several scandals in the US (both men had given up their bonuses in 2002 after that year produced the worst results in the history of CIBC). Kassie afterwards founded Genuity Capital and was alleged to have raided 20 key employees from World Markets for his new startup, causing CIBC to file a lawsuit. Gerald T. McCaughey was named as Kassie's replacement for World Markets. Not long after he was promoted to President and Chief Operating Officer, assuring his succession to CEO, Jill Denham, Vice Chair of Retail Markets and a potential candidate for the CEO post, was reportedly dismissed by McCaughey. Denham was reported close to Hunkin and Kassie and McCaughey wanted to build his own senior executive team.

Executive Team

- Gerald T. McCaughey - President and CEO
- Sonia Baxendale - Senior Executive Vice-President, CIBC and President, CIBC Retail Markets
- Mike Capatides - Chief Administrative Officer and General Counsel, Administration Division, CIBC
- Ron Lalonde - Senior Executive Vice-President, Technology and Operations, CIBC
- Richard Nesbitt - CEO, CIBC World Markets
- Richard E. Venn - Senior Executive Vice-President, Corporate Development, CIBC, Managing Director and Deputy Chairman, CIBC World Markets Inc.
- David Williamson - Senior Executive Vice-President and Chief Financial Officer, CIBC
- Tom Woods - Senior Executive Vice-President and Chief Risk Officer, Risk Management, CIBC

Board of directors

Current members of the board of directors of the company are (as of May 2010):

- Brent S. Belzberg (2005); Senior Managing Partner, Torquest Partners Inc.
- Jalynn H. Bennett (1994) C.M.; President, Jalynn H. Bennett and Associates Ltd.
- Gary F. Colter (2003) F.C.A.; President, CRS Inc.
- Dominic D'Alessandro (2010); Past President and Chief Executive Officer, Manulife Financial Corporation
- Patrick D. Daniel (2009) B.S., M.S. Chem. E; President and Chief Executive Officer, Enbridge Inc.
- Luc Desjardins (2009); Equity Partner, The Sterling Group, LP
- Gordon D. Giffin (2001); Senior Partner, McKenna Long & Aldridge LLP
- Linda S. Hasenfratz (2004); Chief Executive Officer, Linamar Corporation
- Nicholas D. Le Pan (2008); Consultant, 6610587 Canada Inc.
- John P. Manley, P.C. (2005); President and Chief Executive Officer, Canadian Council of Chief Executives
- Gerald T. McCaughey (2005); President and Chief Executive Officer, CIBC

- Jane L. Peverett (2009); Corporate Director
- Leslie Rahl (2007) B.Sc., M.B.A.; Founder and Managing Partner, Capital Market Risk Advisors, Inc.
- Charles Sirois (1997) C.M., B.Fin., M.Fin.; Chair of the Board, CIBC
- Robert J. Steacy (2008); Corporate Director
- Ronald W. Tysoe (2004); Retired Chairman, Macy's, Inc.

Past presidents, CEOs and chairmen

The following is an incomplete list.

Former Canadian Bank of Commerce Presidents

- Hon. William McMaster 1867-1886 - founder of the Canadian Bank of Commerce, Liberal Senator 1867-1887 and founder of McMaster University, former Bank of Montreal director 1864-1867
- **Sir John Aird** 1924-1929 - Chairman of the Royal Commission on Radio Broadcasting
- Sir Byron Edmund Walker 1907-1924
- James Stewart CBE
- William M. Currie
- Neil McKinnon - President 1956-1961

Vice-Presidents

- Robert Winters 1968-1969

Former Imperial Bank of Canada Presidents

- Henry Stark Howland 1875-1889 - founder and former Bank of Commerce VP 1867-1875; former reeve and postmaster for the Village of Kleinburg 1859-1860, York County Warden .
- George Albertus Cox 1890-1896 - Liberal Senator 1896-1914

Chairmen

- Lindsay Stuart Mackersy MC 1961-? - First President of CIBC

Former Canadian Imperial Bank of Commerce Presidents

- Lindsay Stuart Mackersy MC 1961-?
- John S. Hunkin 1999-2004

Chairmen

- Russell Harrison
- Neil MacKinnon
- Donald S Fullerton
- A.L. Flood CM - 1988-1998
- John Hunkin - 1999-2003
- Bill Etherington - 2003-2009
- Charles Sirois 2009–present

CEOs

- John S. Hunkin

  Chief Executive Officer 2004-2005; President and CEO of CIBC 1999-2004; CEO and President of CIBC World Markets 1990-1992, President of Investment and Corporate Banking - CIBC Wood Gundy 1992-1997, President of Investment and Corporate Banking - CIBC World Markets 1997-1999.

Notable former employees

- Paul S. Cantor - member of the Board of Directors of CIBC
- Jill Denham - EVP Wealth Management
- A.L. Flood - former CIBC chair
- John S. Hunkin - CEO of CIBC
- David Kassie - former CEO of CIBC World Markets and now CEO of Genuity Capital Markets
- Holger Kluge - CIBC EVP
- Donald R. Lindsay - former President of CIBC World Markets Inc., and now CEO and Director of Teck Cominco
- William McMaster - founder of the Canadian Bank of Commerce
- Brian Molony - former assistant bank manager who stole more than 9 million U.S. dollars from CIBC and lost all of it gambling.
- Robert W. Service, poet and former clerk with Canadian Bank of Commerce

- Robert Winters - former CIBC Vice-President and federal cabinet minister under Pierre Trudeau
- George Herbert Wood and James Henry Gundy - founders of Wood, Gundy & Company

Controversies

2003: Enron

On December 22, 2003, the Security and Exchange Commission (SEC) fined CIBC US$ 80 million for its role in the manipulation of Enron financial statements. This consists of $37.5 million to repay ill-gotten gains, a $37.5 million penalty and $5 million in interest. The money is intended to be returned to Enron fraud victims pursuant to the Fair Fund provisions of Section 308(a) of the Sarbanes-Oxley Act of 2002.

The SEC also sued three of CIBC's executives. CIBC Executive Vice President Daniel Ferguson and former CIBC Executive Director Mark Wolf agreed to settle for US$ 563,000 and US$ 60,000, respectively. Ian Schottlaender, former managing director in CIBC's corporate leveraged finance group in New York initially contested the charges but on July 12, 2004 he agreed to pay US$ 528,750 as well as be barred from serving as an officer or director of a publicly traded company for a period of five years. Under these agreements the individuals neither admit nor deny wrongdoing.

The SEC complaint charges that "CIBC and the three executives with having helped Enron to mislead its investors through a series of complex structured finance transactions over a period of several years preceding Enron's bankruptcy." The agreement reached between the SEC and CIBC permanently enjoins CIBC from violating the antifraud, books and records, and internal control provisions of the federal securities laws.

On August 2, 2005 CIBC paid US$ 2.4 billion to settle a class action lawsuit brought by a group of pension funds and investment managers, including the University of California, which claims that "systematic fraud by Enron and its officers led to the loss of billions and the collapse of the company."

2003: market timing

On July 25, 2005 CIBC confirmed it would pay US$ 125 million to settle an investigation into its role in the 2003 Mutual-fund scandal. Linda Chatman Thomsen, director of the SEC's division of enforcement, said, "by knowingly financing customers' late trading and market timing, as well as providing financing in amounts far greater than the law allows, CIHI and World Markets boosted their customers' trading profits at the expense of long-term mutual fund shareholders." Under the settlement, CIBC neither admits nor denies the allegations.

2004: CIBC Visa Cardholders

On August 27, 2004 CIBC confirmed that it would settle a class-action lawsuit on behalf of CIBC Visa cardholders. The plaintiffs, represented by Paul Pape and Harvey Strosberg of the Toronto law firm Pape Barristers, alleged that the conversion of foreign-currency transactions resulted in an undisclosed or inadequately disclosed mark-up. After having been approved by an Ontario Superior Court judge, CIBC announced on October 15, 2004 that the settlement will result in the bank paying $13.85 million to its cardholders, $1 million to the United Way, $1.65 million to the Class Action Fund of the Law Society of Upper Canada (Ontario), and $3 million in legal fees. The bank also announced that it has not admitted any liability and is settling to avoid further litigation with its cardholders.

2004: Erroneous Charges

On May 20, 2004 CIBC announced that it would refund $24 million to some of its customers as a result of erroneous overdraft and mortgage charges which were discovered in the course of an internal review. "This is being done as part of CIBC's effort to correct its error and to ensure that it distributes to customers all of the money it received in error," the bank said.

In another similar incident, CIBC announced on April 27, 2006 that it's refunding an additional $27 million to about 200,000 clients who were overcharged for certain overdraft fees and other borrowing transactions, some of which date back to 1993. In cases where clients were undercharged, the bank decided not to seek reimbursement.

2005: Privacy

On April 18, 2005 the Privacy Commissioner of Canada expressed disappointment in the way CIBC dealt with incidents involving the bank misdirecting faxes containing customers' personal information. One involved misdirecting faxes to a scrap yard operator in West Virginia from 2001 to 2004. The misdirected faxes contained the social security numbers, home addresses, phone numbers, and detailed bank account data of several hundred bank customers.

The second incident involved a Dorval businessman and allegedly took place from 2000 to 2004. In both cases, the commissioner noted that the bank did not inform the affected clients, whose personal information was compromised, until the incidents became public and an investigation was underway.

A few days after the story broke on CTV News and The Globe and Mail, CIBC announced that it had banned its employees from using fax machines to transmit any documents containing confidential customer information.

2007: Privacy

On January 18, 2007 CIBC Asset Management announced that the personal information of about 470,000 current and former clients of Talvest Mutual Funds, a CIBC subsidiary, had gone missing. The information may have included client names, addresses, signatures, dates of birth, bank account numbers, beneficiary information and/or Social Insurance Numbers. The incident emanated from the disappearance of a hard drive containing information on "the process used to open and administer" customer accounts as it was traveling between the bank's Montreal and Toronto offices. The Privacy Commissioner of Canada stated, "Although I appreciate that the bank notified us of this incident and that it is working cooperatively with my Office, I am nevertheless deeply troubled, especially given the magnitude of this breach, which puts at risk the personal information of hundreds of thousands of Canadians." She immediately launched a privacy investigation.

2007: Employee Overtime

In June 2007, CIBC was named in a $600 million class-action lawsuit regarding the lack of overtime pay to its customer service staff. The lawsuit was launched by Dara Fresco, a head teller at the bank, who is being represented by the law firms Roy Elliot Kim O'Connor LLP and Sack Goldblatt Mitchell LLP. A class-action case management judge is being assigned to the case and the class-action certification is being assessed - a process that could take up to one year. The case was recently dismissed by Madam Justice Joan Lax of the Ontario Superior Court where she stated the evidence "provides no basis in fact that there is a systemic practice of unpaid overtime at CIBC."

Unionization

Currently only select branches are unionized. The Sudbury branch staff and CIBC VISA department are part of the powerful United Steelworkers union.

Significant buildings occupied by CIBC

- Commerce Court
- Tour CIBC
- 2 Bloor Street West
- 20 Exchange Place-CIBC Building, New York
- CIBC 750 Lawrence
- Bankers Hall East
- Bell Trinity Square
- Brookfield Place

Notes

Li Ka Shing, Hong Kong billionaire was the largest foreign shareholder in the bank for over two decades, but in early 2005 he sold his portion (est. C$1.2 billion) to establish a Canadian charity, the Li Ka Shing Foundation. CIBC was Mr. Li's choice for financing many of his Canadian ventures, like Husky Energy. Mr. Li had reportedly backed personal and commercial banking head Holger Kluge to succeed Al Flood as CEO of CIBC in 1999.

References

- Victor Ross *A History of the Canadian Bank of Commerce* (1920–1934)
- Rupert *Canadian Investment Bank Review* McGraw-Hill Ryerson, Limited 1992

External links

Personal Banking Websites

- CIBC Official Website [1]
- CIBC Imperial Service [2]
- CIBC Wood Gundy [3]
- CIBC Private Wealth Management [4]
- CIBC Investor's Edge [5]
- CIBC Asian Banking [6]
- CIBC Mobile Banking (www.cibc.mobi) [7]

Business & Corporate Banking Websites

- CIBC Small Business [8]
- CIBC Commercial Banking [9]
- CIBC Large Corporate Banking [10]
- Wholesale Banking [11]
- CIBC Mellon [12]
- CIBC Asset Management [13]

Related Websites

- FirstCaribbean International Bank (CIBC-Caribbean Region) [14]
- President's Choice Financial Home Page [15]
- FirstLine Mortgages [16]
- HLC Home Loans Canada [17]
- Renaissance Investments [18]

CIBC stock profiles and quotes

Canada

- CIBC TSX Stock Quote [19]
- Google finance Canada - Canadian Imperial Bank of Commerce [20]
- CIBC Investor Relations [21]

USA

- CIBC NYSE Stock Quote [22]
- CIBC stock performance chart [23] from GStock
- Google finance - Canadian Imperial Bank of Commerce (USA) [24]

Notable Second Tier Banks

National Bank of Canada

Type	Public company TSX: NA [1]
Industry	Bank
Founded	Montreal, Quebec, Canada 1859
Headquarters	Montreal, Quebec, Canada
Key people	Louis Vachon (CEO)
Products	Financial services
Revenue	$4.1 billion CAD (2009)
Net income	▲ $854 million CAD (2009)
Total assets	$132.1 billion CAD (2009)
Employees	14,851 (Full-time equivalent, 2009)
Website	www.nbc.ca [4]

National Bank of Canada (*Banque Nationale du Canada*) (TSX: NA [1]) is the 6th largest bank and 8th largest financial institution (by market cap) in Canada. The bank's headquarters are in Montreal, Quebec. There are 446 branches, the vast majority of which are in Quebec, Ontario and New Brunswick, and 2.35 million personal clients. The bank also has representative offices or branches in Havana, Hong Kong, London, Paris, Nassau, New York City, and a subsidiary of 2 branches in Florida named Natbank. National Bank of Canada's Institution Number (or bank number) is 006.

The bank is mainly used by French-speaking Canadians, with the majority of bank branches being centred in the province of Quebec.

Services

Personal and Commercial	Wealth Management	Financial Markets
• In-branch and remote payment services for individuals and businesses • Broad offering of mortgage and personal loan products for consumers • Full suite of savings and investment products sold through specialists in the branches and business offices • Banking products marketed through partnerships • Lending, deposit and cash management services for businesses • Specialized financing: oil and gas, agribusiness, audio-visual productions, health • International foreign exchange, factoring and payment services • Credit cards for consumers and businesses • Point-of-sale financing • Direct sale of automobile and home insurance • Sale of group insurance products to businesses • Life and health insurance products • Financial and estate planning services • Private Banking	• Full-service and discount brokerage • Trust and custodial services • Design, management and support for sales of products marketed through the branches such as National Bank Mutual Funds and Private Investment Management • Institutional investment portfolio management • Administrative services for third-party brokers • Design and marketing of investment products to third parties and direct sale of mutual funds	• Financing through equities, bonds and credit facilities • Deposit, foreign exchange and riskmanagement services to corporations, governments and institutional clients • Merger and acquisition advisory services • Investing on the Bank's behalf • Design of structured products for consumers and personalized solutions for high-net-worth clients • Trading on capital markets: shares, fixed-income securities, derivatives, foreign exchange and commodities • Bank financing and asset/liability matching • Alternative management

History

- 1859: Eugène Chinic, Isodore Thibodeau, Ulric-Joseph Tessier, Olivier Robitaille, Cirice Têtu, David Dussault, Prudent Vallée and other citizens of Quebec decide to create the Banque Nationale, an institution by and for the francophone community. The legislature permits the bank to incorporate.
- 1860: Banque Nationale commences operations.
- 1924: Banque Nationale is caught up in a serious recession. It merges with Banque d'Hochelaga (est. in Montréal in 1874) to form Banque Canadienne Nationale (BCN).
- 1976: BCN establishes an agency in New York.
- 1979: BCN merges with the Provincial Bank of Canada/Banque provinciale du Canada to form the Banque Nationale du Canada (BNC; National Bank of Canada).
- 1983: The New York agency becomes a branch, and the bank opens a representative office in Seoul.
- 1985: BNC acquires Mercantile Bank of Canada from Citibank. Mercantile has an office in New York (licensed 1984), which BNC merges in.
- 1987: BNC swaps US$4 million of restructured bad loans for one-tenth of Banco Osorno y La Union, a Chilean bank.
- 1988: BNC acquired the stock brokerage firm, Lévesque, Beaubien Inc., now known as National Bank Financial
- 1993: BNC acquires the assets of General Trust of Canada (established 1927).
- 1994: BNC establishes a US subsidiary, Natbank, with a branch in Pompano Beach in Florida. BNC also establishes a representative office in Mexico City.
- 1995: Natbank opens its second branch and a head office in Hollywood, Florida. BNC opens an office in Havana in response to the passage of a new law in Cuba authorizing foreign bank representative offices.
- 1996: BNC acquires Family Trust Corporation and The Municipal Savings & Loans Corporation, both in Ontario. Also, BNC sells its stake in Banco Osorno y la Union to Banco Santander, which acquires the bank.
- 2001: BNC acquires 17 branches in Quebec from Bank of Montreal.
- 2008: Altamira and National Bank announce they will be merging Altamira operations into NBC branches.

BNC closed the offices in Beirut, Mexico City, Seoul, Shanghai, and Taipei that it managed at various times.

Membership

The National Bank of Canada is a member of the Canadian Bankers Association (CBA) and registered member with the Canada Deposit Insurance Corporation (CDIC), a federal agency insuring deposits at all of Canada's chartered banks. It is also a member of:

- Cirrus Network
- Interac
- MasterCard International
- NYCE point of sale Network
- The Exchange (Canada)

See also List of banks in Canada

Key subsidiaries

- National Bank Home and Auto Insurance
- Credigy Services Corporation-defaulted credit card debt collector
- Credigy Receivables, Inc.-buyer of defaulted credit card accounts

Corporate governance

Current members of the board of directors of the National Bank of Canada are: Lawrence Bloomberg, Pierre Bourgie, Gérard Coulombe, Bernard Cyr, Shirley Dawe, Nicole Diamond-Gélinas, Jean Douville, Marcel Dutil, Jean Gaulin, Paul Gobeil, Réal Raymond, Roseann Runte, and Marc Tellier.

External links

- National Bank of Canada/Banque Nationale du Canada [4]
- National Bank Insurance [2]

Desjardins Group

Type	Cooperative
Industry	Financial services
Founded	Lévis, Québec, Canada (1900)
Headquarters	Lévis, Québec and Montréal, Québec, Canada
Key people	Monique Leroux, President & Chief Executive Officer
Products	Chequing Accounts Insurance stock brokerage Investment Bank Asset-Based Lending Consumer finance
Employees	39,985 (2006)
Website	www.desjardins.com [1]

The **Desjardins Group** (or **Mouvement des caisses Desjardins** in French) is the largest association of credit unions in North America. It was founded in 1900 in Lévis, Québec by Alphonse Desjardins.

A Desjardins Credit Union in Toronto, Ontario.

Located mostly in Québec as well as in Ontario, Manitoba, and New Brunswick, it is composed of 536 local *caisses populaires,* which serve 5.8 million members. The entire system is grouped into 11 regional federations.

Total assets at Desjardins Group reached $151.9 billion CAD in 2008, ranking it the sixth-largest financial institution in Canada and the largest in Québec, ahead of National Bank of Canada. It had in 2006 over 40 000 employees and 6 500 elected and volunteer officers. In 2006, it gave its members $483 million CAD in patronage allocations and $64 million CAD in donations, sponsorships and academic scholarships. Most of the latter sum was used on regional economic development and health programs as well.

The Desjardins Group has over 20 subsidiaries, ranging from insurance services (Desjardins Financial Security, Desjardins General Insurance), real estate (Place Desjardins), venture capital funds

(Desjardins Venture Capital) and brokerage services (Desjardins Securities). The Desjardins Group, through its subsidiary Développement international Desjardins, is also active in over 50 developing countries through technical assistance programs and various investments.

Desjardins Group is currently expanding outside the province of Quebec: in 1992 it opened the Desjardins Bank in Florida to cater to southbound Quebecers, particularly snowbirds and retirees; this latter practice has also been adopted by a number of the banks in Canada.

Desjardins is a member of:

- Interac
- NYCE ATM Network

See also

- Complexe Desjardins
- Credit union

External links

- Desjardins Group [2] website

HSBC Bank Canada

Type	Subsidiary of HSBC Holdings plc
Industry	Finance and Insurance
Founded	1981
Headquarters	Vancouver, British Columbia, Canada
Key people	Michael Geoghegan, Chairman Lindsay Gordon, President and CEO
Products	Financial Services
Employees	6,000
Website	www.hsbc.ca [1]

HSBC Bank Canada, formerly the **Hongkong Bank of Canada**, is a bank in Canada that is part of British banking giant HSBC - one of the largest banking groups in the world. HSBC Canada is the seventh largest bank in Canada, with offices in every province except Prince Edward Island, and is the largest foreign-owned bank in the country. Corporate headquarters are in the financial district of Vancouver, British Columbia.

History

HSBC Bank Canada headquarters in Vancouver, Canada.

In 1979, The Hongkong and Shanghai Banking Corporation bought a Vancouver-based acceptance company that financed machinery and equipment for small companies operating in British Columbia. In 1981, The Hongkong and Shanghai Banking Corporation incorporated Hongkong Bank of Canada (HBC), in Vancouver as a chartered bank effective July 1, 1981 under the Bank Act of Canada. HBC used the acceptance company as a base for the new bank. HBC had a few retail branches primarily focused on Asian-Canadians, but the major portion of the bank's business was with commercial enterprises. HBC opened branches in major cities in western Canada and in Toronto and Montreal but growth was slow. HBC sought to grow by acquisition, but the first three attempts to buy an existing institution were unsuccessful. In 1986, on November 27, HBC acquired the assets of

An HSBC branch in Markham, Ontario.

Bank of British Columbia, which had essentially failed. HBC gained $2.6 billion in assets and added 41 branches in British Columbia and Alberta. Overnight, HBC moved from the 20th largest to 9th largest bank in Canada.

In 1988, on May 20, HBC amalgamated with Midland Bank Canada, thereby increasing assets by $472 million, gaining many new corporate banking relationships, and expanding to Eastern Canada. In 1990, on May 29, HBC acquired Lloyds Bank of Canada, thereby increasing assets by $4.4 billion and adding 53 branches across Canada, mostly in Ontario and Quebec. HBC's assets after this acquisition were $10.2 billion at October 31, 1990. This merger doubled its branch network, substantially increased HBC's exposure in eastern Canada, and made it a bilingual operation with branches in eight Quebec communities. HBC became the largest foreign bank. (Lloyds Bank had acquired Continental Bank of Canada 1986. This began in 1973 as Niagara Finance Company, became IAC Limited, and then Continental Bank.) In 1993, on April 30, HBC acquired ANZ Canada consisting of one office in Toronto, which it merged with its 70 York Street branch. This purchase made HBC the seventh largest bank in Canada with branches in every province except Prince Edward Island. (ANZ had acquired Grindlays Bank Canada with its acquisition of Grindlays, but management was more interested in expanding in the Asia-Pacific area.) In 1995, on August 1, HBC acquired Metropolitan Trust Company of Canada (1 branch).

In 1996, on August 31, HBC acquired Barclays Bank Canada. Barclays had re-entered Canada in 1979 and developed a diversified but modest range of activities. In 1985, it bought the assets of Wells Fargo Bank (Canada). Wells Fargo sold its operations in Alberta (and in Florida) to Barclays as part of a re-focusing on its home market. In 1993, Barclays Bank Canada closed its Edmonton branch. In 1994, Barclays closed six branches (Vancouver, Calgary, Winnipeg, London, Montreal and Halifax), retaining only its head office. Barclays' Canadian operations lost approximately $120-million between 1992 and 1996. HBC acquires the Seattle, Washington and Portland, Oregon branches of HSBC. The growing north-south trade occasioned by the adoption of the North American Free Trade Agreement (NAFTA) in 1994 made this move into the United States seem a natural expansion along with the business interests of many of the bank's customers. In 1998, on May 1, HBC acquired National Westminster Bank of Canada, which had assets of C$844.5 million. NatWest had entered Canada in 1982. In 1999, on June 21, HBC changed its name to HSBC Bank Canada, consistent with the HSBC Group's strategy of creating the global brand, HSBC. On December 3, it acquired Prenor Trust Company of Canada.

In 2000, HSBC Bank Canada acquired Republic National Bank of New York (Canada) after HSBC acquired the parent bank. (Republic had entered Canada in 1982, and had itself acquired several banks. First, in 1993, Republic acquired Bank Leumi Le Israel (Canada). The next year, Republic bought

Israel-based Bank Hapoalim (Canada). Lastly, in 1996, Republic bought Israel Discount Bank of Canada's operations.) In 2001, on April 1, HSBC (Canada) acquired CCF Canada after HSBC acquired CCF Canada's parent company, CCF. CCF had just acquired Crédit Lyonnais Canada. Credit Commercial de France (Canada) had entered Canada in 1982 when it established an office in Montreal. Société Genérale (Canada) acquired it in 1990. CCF had returned to Canada in 2000. In 2002, HSBC Holdings merged its Canadian and US operations to create a North American transnational bank. HSBC Bank USA of New York, with assets of US$87 billion, and HSBC Canada, with assets of C$34 billion, share some operating resources but remain separate units. In 2004, HSBC Bank Canada acquired Intesa Bank's Canadian unit, which had 11 branches and total assets of C$1.1 billion when the two banks completed the transaction on June 1, 2004.

Divisions

Operating divisions of HSBC:

- HSBC Investments (Canada)
- HSBC Capital (Canada)
- HSBC Trust Company (Canada)
- HSBC Securities (Canada), which includes a discount brokerage division called HSBC InvestDirect
- HSBC Insurance Agency (Canada)

Executives

- Lindsay Gordon, president and chief executive officer
- Matthew M Bosrock - deputy chief executive officer
- Brad J Meredith, executive vice president, global banking and markets
- Margaret Willis, executive vice president personal financial services
- Vacant, executive vice president commercial banking
- Graham McIsaac, chief financial officer
- Bob Anthony, chief credit officer
- Neal Beasley, chief information officer
- Scott Bartos, chief compliance officer

Sponsorships

- Toronto Blue Jays Baseball Club
- Vancouver Canucks Hockey Club
- Calgary Flames Hockey Club
- HSBC Celebration of Light - An annual international fireworks show in Vancouver, BC
- MMICC - McGill Management International Case Competition in Montreal, QC
- Jetbridges at Toronto Pearson International Airport

Membership

HSBC Canada is a member of the Canadian Bankers Association (CBA) and registered member with the Canada Deposit Insurance Corporation (CDIC), a federal agency insuring deposits at all of Canada's chartered banks. It is also a member of:

- Interac
- MasterCard
- Cirrus Network
- The Exchange

Effective March 15, 2010, BMO Bank of Montreal ceased accepting deposits at its ATMs from HSBC customers and resumed charging a convenience fee after five years of an ATM sharing agreement with HSBC Bank Canada. HSBC continues as a member of The Exchange Network. This was a decision HSBC took as part of a restructuring of its personal banking strategy. Instead, HSBC will rebate the convenience fee charged to its HSBC Premier qualified customers to a maximum of $1.50 per instance for using any ATM in Canada.

See also

- List of Canadian banks

External links

- Official site [2]
- HSBC site [3]

ING Group

Type	Naamloze vennootschap (Euronext: INGA [1], NYSE: ING [2])
Industry	Financial services
Founded	1991
Headquarters	Amsterdam, Netherlands
Area served	Worldwide
Key people	Jan Hommen (CEO), Patrick Flynn (CFO), Peter Elverding (Chairman of the supervisory board)
Products	Retail, direct, private, investment and commercial banking, insurance and asset management
Revenue	€48.19 billion (2009)
Profit	▼ (€935 million) (2009)
Total assets	€1.164 trillion (2009)
Total equity	€39.778 billion (2009)
Employees	107,000 (FTE, 2009)
Website	www.ing.com [3]

ING Group (Euronext: INGA [1], NYSE: ING [2]) is a financial institution of Dutch origin offering banking, insurance and asset management services. *ING* is an abbreviation of **Internationale Nederlanden Groep** (English: *International Netherlands Group*).

As of 2009, ING Group serves 85 million private, corporate and institutional clients in over 40 countries, with a workforce of over 100,000 people. It owns ING Direct, a virtual bank, as well as retail banking, insurance, investment management, and investment banking operations. Its services operate in countries including Australia, Canada, France, India, Italy, New Zealand, Spain, Poland, UK, and the US. ING is the largest banking/financial company in the world by revenue.

International operations

ING has offices in:

- Argentina
- Australia
- Austria
- Belarus
- Belgium
- Brazil
- Bulgaria
- Canada
- Chile

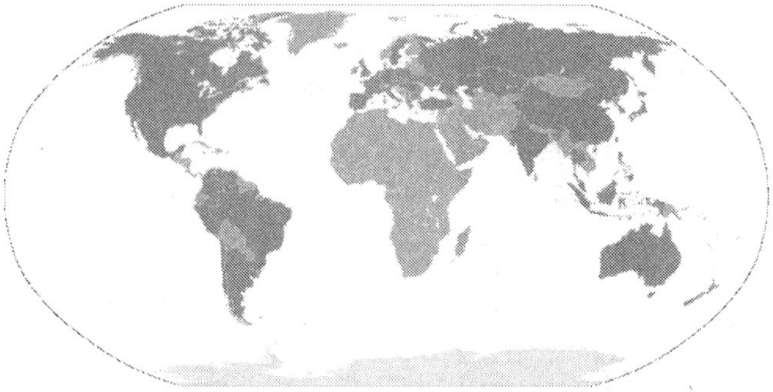

ING Group global locations

- China
- Colombia
- Czech Republic
- France
- Germany
- Greece
- Hong Kong
- Hungary
- India
- Indonesia
- Italy
- Japan
- Malaysia
- Mexico
- Mongolia
- The Netherlands
- New Zealand
- Luxembourg
- Peru
- Philippines
- Poland
- Romania
- Russia
- Singapore
- Slovakia

- South Korea
- Spain
- Taiwan
- Turkey
- Thailand
- Ukraine
- United Arab Emirates
- United Kingdom
- United States

Headquarters

ING's headquarters, ING House, is located in the business district of Zuidas in Amsterdam. It was designed by Roberto Meyer and Jeroen van Schooten and was officially opened on 16 September 2002 by Prince Willem-Alexander of the Netherlands. The light-infused building features a 250 seat auditorium, foyer, restaurant, and library, and is also home to an art collection.

ING House, ING headquarters in Amsterdam

History

- 1991: The newly formed company, first called Internationale Nederlanden Groep, later ING Group, was created from the merger of Nationale-Nederlanden and NMB Postbank Group.
- 1991: Nationale-Nederlanden changes to ING Nationale-Nederlanden
- 1991: ING financial group entered the Czech market
- 1994: ING opened first ING Bank in Romania
- 1995: ING acquired investment bank and investment management firm Barings after its collapse (in the process, it also obtained the original sales document of the Louisiana Purchase)
- 1997: ING acquired insurer Equitable of Iowa Companies
- 1997: ING opened ING Direct Canada www.ingdirect.ca
- 1998: ING acquired Banque Bruxelles Lambert (BBL) of Belgium
- 1999: ING acquired BHF-Bank of Germany, opened ING Direct Spain
- 2000: ING acquired US insurers ReliaStar, Aetna Financial Services and Aetna International
- 2000: ING opened ING Direct USA
- 2001: ING acquired Bank Śląski of Poland, and insurer Seguros Comercial America of Mexico
- 2002: ING acquired DiBa bank of Germany

- 2003: ING opened ING Direct UK
- 2004: ING Insurance Company of Canada acquired Allianz Canada
- 2004: ING sold BHF-Bank of Germany to Sal. Oppenheim
- 2005: ING ordered to pay $1.5 million by the NASD for permitting improper market timing in ING funds.
- 2005: ING acquired a 19.9% stake in Bank of Beijing; which was later diluted to 16.07% after the company listed in Shanghai
- 2006: ING opened ING Life Bulgaria, a branch of ING Life Hungary
- 2007: ING acquired the domestic asset management operations of ABN AMRO Asset Management in Taiwan
- 2007: ING acquired Oyak bank of Turkey
- 2007: ING launched its first variable annuities product for the European market in Spain
- 2007: ING acquired US web-based stock brokerage firm ShareBuilder
- 2007: ING acquired Landmark Asset Management Company of South Korea
- 2007: ING acquired a 30% stake in TMB Bank, Thailand
- 2007: ING acquired NetBank when NetBank was closed by the US Office of Thrift Supervision
- 2007: Ernst and Young became registered independent auditors of ING Group
- 2008: ING sold ING Seguros in Mexico
- 2008: ING acquired CitiStreet in the USA
- 2008: ING launched retail banking in Ukraine
- 2008: ING acquired the voluntary pension fund Oyak Emeklilik in Turkey
- 2008: ING sold its life insurance business in Taiwan
- 2008: ING Group, in a move to increase its Tier-One capital ratio, accepts a €10 billion capital injection from the Dutch government.
- 2009: ING closed retail banking in Ukraine
- 2009: In order to save €1.4 billion, ING announced that they would be cutting about 7,000 employees from their payroll. The CEO, Michel Tilmant, also resigned.
- 2009: ING Group sold all of its ownership stake in ING Canada (Property & Casualty Insurer operating in Canada).
- 2009: ING Group's Restructuring Plan announced, stating that ING needs to divest ING Direct USA by the end of 2013.
- 2009: ING announces that it will move towards a separation of its banking and insurance operations.
- 2009: ING secures €7.5bn rights issue and repays €5bn to the Dutch State.

Transactions with the Dutch State

Capital injection

Part of ING at night in Minneapolis, Minnesota in the United States

On Sunday October 19, 2008, in a move to increase its core Tier 1 capital ratio to above 8%, ING Group accepted a capital injection plan by the Dutch Government. The plan will supply €10 billion (US$13.5 billion) into the operation, in exchange for securities, and veto rights on major operations and investments. Wouter Bos, the Dutch finance minister at the time, said that this was done as a means of fortifying the bank as the bank is in a sound financial state, to weather the financial crisis. Management said that the capital injection shall have no dilutive impact to existing shareholders. As part of the 'loan' agreement, two government advisers have been appointed to the supervisory board.

Repayment of Dutch state

On 21 Dec 2009, ING announced that it has completed its planned repurchase of EUR 5 billion of the Core Tier 1 securities issued in November 2008 to the Dutch State and its EUR 7.5 billion rights issue.

Divisions

Retail Banking

ING offers retail banking services in the Netherlands, Belgium, Luxembourg, Poland, Romania, Turkey, India, Thailand and China. Private Banking is offered in the Netherlands, Belgium, Luxembourg, Switzerland and various countries in Asia and Central Europe. Mid Corporate Clients in the home markets (the Netherlands, Belgium, Poland and Romania) are also part of Retail Banking.

In its home market, the Netherlands, ING is the largest retail bank by market share, holding 40% of current account deposits [4], followed by Rabobank (30%), ABN AMRO (20%), and others (10%).

Outside of the Benelux, ING's focus is on Central and Eastern Europe, and Asia. In India, ING has a 44% stake in ING Vysya Bank and is the single largest shareholder. In China, ING has a 16.7% stake in Bank of Beijing, the largest city commercial bank in China. In Thailand, ING has a 30% stake in TMB Bank, a universal banking platform with a nationwide network.

ING Direct

ING Direct is ING Group's marketing name for a branchless direct bank with operations in Australia, Austria (branded *ING-DiBa*), Canada, France, Germany (branded *ING-DiBa*), Italy, Spain, the United Kingdom and the United States. It offers services over the Internet, phone, ATM or by mail, and focuses on simple, high-interest savings accounts.

ING Direct Canada

ING Direct Canada was founded in 1997. As of 2009 ING DIRECT Canada has over 1.6 million clients, employs over 900 people and has over $27 billion in assets. ING Direct Canada has four 'Save Your Money Cafés' in the major cities of Toronto, Montréal, Calgary and Vancouver.

Its products include Savings accounts, Tax-Free Savings Accounts (TFSAs), Mortgages, Retirement Savings Plans (RSPs), Guaranteed Investments (GICs), Mutual Funds, and Business Accounts.

ING Direct Canada is a member of the Canadian Bankers Association **(CBA)** and registered member with the Canada Deposit Insurance Corporation **(CDIC)**, a federal agency insuring deposits at all of Canada's chartered banks. ING Direct Canada operates as Banking Institution #614, Transit #00152.

ING Direct United States

ING Direct was founded in 2000, with its headquarters in Wilmington, Delaware. ING Direct is a member of the Federal Deposit Insurance Corporation (FDIC).

In September 2007, ING Direct acquired 104,000 customers and FDIC insured assets from a failed virtual bank NetBank. Two months later, ING Direct acquired online stock broker Sharebuilder.

Orange Savings Account

Its product range includes Savings, checking, IRA, and CDs accounts The Orange Savings Account is an online savings product offered by ING Direct. ING Direct allows users two possible methods to deposit money into an Orange Savings account: electronic transfer from a checking account at another institution, and direct deposit. Customers can link up to three external checking accounts for electronic deposits and withdrawals.

Individual Retirement (IRA) Savings Account

Traditional and Roth IRA accounts are offered. Both are near paperless products. Accounts can be opened online, in addition to supporting contributions and distributions without forms. Only bank to bank custodial transfers and conversions require paperwork. Rates follow the rates of the OSA. Customers may also open IRA CDs that are tied to their IRA savings account.

Electric Orange Checking

Electric Orange is ING Direct's interest-bearing paperless checking account. The account has no minimum balance or direct deposit requirements, no monthly maintenance fees, and pays tiered interest rate according to account balance. Access to the account is available through a MasterCard debit card (withdrawals at Allpoint ATMs are free), "Electric Checks" which are electronic transfers to other people who don't need to be ING Direct account holders, free Bill Pay, and direct debit. Unlike a traditional checking account, Electric Orange account does not allow access via paper checks written by the account holder, although customers can request ING Direct to print and mail a check on the account holder's behalf. Checks mailed by ING Direct are debited from the account at the moment of the request and regardless whether the check is ever cashed. Deposit options include Automated Clearing House (ACH) transfers from a linked account at another bank, direct deposit, transfer from Orange Savings accounts as well as mailing in paper checks. Foreign transactions are subject to a 3% fee. Unlike the Orange Savings Account, enrollment in ING Direct's "e1st" program is mandatory for Electronic Orange customers, and the account holder of an Electronic Orange account must agree to receive information about all their ING Direct accounts electronically through the Internet. Customers that do not have an Electric Orange account may still opt to have paper statements mailed to them. Also, unlike the Orange Savings Account, the Electric Orange account offers overdraft protection, this is however, mandatory, if you do not have the necessary credit, you will be not be allowed to open an Electric Orange account.

Orange Certificate of Deposit

Another popular savings method that ING Direct offers is a certificate of deposit, or CD. ING Direct offers a number of options for their CDs, with the time starting out at a minimum of six months, and the longest being 60 months. These products are also offered within IRA savings accounts.

ING Direct Cafes

In March 2001, ING Direct opened cafés in 6 cities: Chicago, IL, Philadelphia, PA, Los Angeles, CA, New York City, NY, St. Cloud, MN, and Wilmington, DE, each serving Peet's Coffee. New cafes were opened in Chicago, IL (Summer 2007), St. Cloud, MN (2008), and Waikiki, Honolulu, Hawai'i (November 2008).

ING Direct Café in New York

Inside the cafés, ING DIRECT has internet terminals that let their account-holders check the status of their ING Direct accounts and surf the Internet free of charge. The cafés often feature seminars on financial topics such as money management, handling one's retirement, mortgages, and credit management.

ING Direct Café in St. Cloud, MN, USA

Services

ING Direct (USA) offers a range of products including Checking accounts, Savings accounts, Business accounts, Mutual funds, and Mortgages.

ING Direct UK

ING Direct began operations in the UK in May 2003 and has over 1 million customers. Operations are based in Reading, where the company head office is situated as well as an office based in the city of Cardiff. The bank markets itself as offering good customer service and high interest rates, which are usually higher than its high street competitors, but not always top of comparison tables. The bank has picked up awards for its customer services and mortgage product in 2008 and 2009.

On 8 October 2008 ING purchased the savings accounts of the collapsed Icelandic bank, Kaupthing Singer & Friedlander, the UK Treasury used the Banking (Special Provisions) Act 2008 to transfer the Kaupthing Edge deposit business to ING Direct. Through this, ING Direct took over responsibility for £2.5 billion of deposits of 160,000 UK customers with the Icelandic bank Kaupthing Edge. Some customers were dissatisfied after ING lowered the exceptional high rate the collapsed Kaupthing was previously paying.

ING Directs products in the UK include Savings Accounts, Cash ISAs, Mortgages and Home insurance.

ING Direct Australia

ING Direct Australia was established in 1999 and is headquartered in Sydney, offering banking online and via telephone.

The company's operations are regulated by the Australian Prudential Regulation Authority and the Australian Securities and Investments Commission, Federal Government regulators. ING Direct is a division of ING Bank (Australia).

In October 2008, ING Direct suffered a $749 million outflow of deposit funds. There had been some confusion as to whether or not the Australian Government's guarantee over funds on deposit applied to deposits up to $1 million with ING DIRECT Australia. Once it was confirmed that the Guarantee did apply to ING DIRECT Australia, outflows that had been solely attributed to this situation slowed and deposits returned.

Its products in Australia include Transaction accounts, Savings accounts, Business accounts, Term deposits and Home loans.

Commercial Banking

ING Commercial Banking conducts operations for corporations and other institutions. The primary focus of ING's Commercial banking business is on the Netherlands, Belgium, Poland and Romania, where it offers a full range of products, from cash management to corporate finance. Elsewhere, it takes a more selective approach to clients and products.

ING Commercial Banking, London office

ING's Commercial Banking business was strengthened in 1995, when ING took over Barings Bank. This acquisition increased the brand recognition of ING around the world and strengthened its Commercial Banking presence in the emerging markets. Following the acquisition and up until 2004, ING's investment banking division was called ING Barings, at which point it severed its ties with the Barings name and was combined with ING's other commercial banking operations. However the top floor of ING's London office is still home to the Baring Art Collection, and the Baring Foundation, a charitable foundation.

Commercial Banking is divided into a number of sub-divisions, including Structured Finance, Financial Markets, and Corporate Finance.

Corporate Finance

ING's Corporate Finance department advises businesses on important corporate transactions, including mergers and acquisitions, initial public offerings, secondary offerings, share buy-backs and management buy-outs. The division is headed by former BP executive, David Herbert, and has made recent key hires from other banks including Maurits Duynstee, previously a Managing Director with ABN AMRO, and now head of ING Corporate Finance for Continental Western Europe. The bank has advised on a number of recent high-profile European transactions including satellite navigation manufacturer TomTom in a €359m rights issue, energy supplier Nuon in its €8.5bn sale to Vattenfall, and printer-maker Océ in its €1.3bn merger with Canon. ING was the leading advisor in the Dutch M&A league tables in 2009.

ING Corporate finance also has a strong presence in Russia and Central and Eastern Europe, where the division is headed by Alexander Kabanovsky and Siobhan Walker. In 2009 ING advised Mobile TeleSystems OJSC (MTS), Russias largest mobile operator, in its acquisition of a 51% stake in

Comstar UTS for USD 1.27bn, and Russia-focused oil producer, Exillon Energy on its USD 100m IPO.

Insurance

ING insurance operates throughout America, Asia and Europe.

In 2009 ING announced plans to separate its insurance business from its main banking operations through an IPO. Analysts estimate that the insurance arm is worth up to €16bn.

Advertising and sponsorship

ING sponsors a variety of sports, cultural events, and art exhibitions throughout the world.

For several years, ING has been the title sponsor of various US Marathons including the New York City Marathon, the Miami Marathon, the Georgia Marathon, the Hartford Marathon, the Philadelphia Distance Run and San Francisco's Bay to Breakers.

ING New York City Marthon

ING is a major sponsor of football, sponsoring the Royal Dutch Football Association and the Asian Football Confederation (AFC).

ING was the title sponsor of the Renault Formula One team from the 2007 season to the 2009 season. It was also during this time, the title sponsor of the Australian Grand Prix and Belgian Grand Prix, the Hungarian Grand Prix, and the Turkish Grand Prix. ING ended its sponsorship of Renault in part due to a reduction in advetising spending, and in part due to controversy surrounding the Renault Formula One team.

In art and culture, ING's sponsorships include the Dutch national museum in Amsterdam (the Rijksmuseum), the New York Museum of Modern Art, and also the Royal Concertgebouw Orchestra. ING also owns a number of collections itself, in Belgium, Mexico, the Netherlands, Poland and the United Kingdom.

ING's use of orange in its corporate logo (as well as including Orange in the name of its products) refers to its Dutch origins. ING's Canadian commercials feature Dutch actor Frederik de Groot. In Australia, they feature Scottish comedian Billy Connolly.

See also

- Australian real estate investment trust
- European Financial Services Roundtable
- Inter-Alpha Group of Banks

External links

ING Websites

- ING.com [3] ING Group mobile [5]
- ING Commercial Banking [6]
- ING Real Estate [7]
- ING USA (www.ing-usa.com) [8]
- ING Asia (www.ing.asia) [9]
- ING DiBa Austria (www.ing-diba.at) [10]

Other websites

- ING Group Headquarters, Galinsky architecture database [11]
- ING Direct U.S. rate history (2001-present) [12]

Regulation

Canada Bank Act

Bank Act	

An Act respecting banks and banking	
Citation	Bank Act [1]
Enacted by	Parliament of Canada
Date assented to	December 13, 1991

The **Bank Act** (1991, c. 46) is an Act of the Government of Canada respecting banks and banking.

The Act groups banks in three schedules. Schedule I banks are banks allowed to accept deposits that are not a subsidiary of a foreign bank, Schedule II banks are banks allowed to accept deposits that are a subsidiary of a foreign bank with branches in Canada, and Schedule III banks are foreign banks with certain restrictions that can do banking business in Canada.

The Bank Act was originally passed in 1871. The terms of the Act provide that it is renewed decennially to ensure that legislators will periodically update the Act in order to keep pace with developments in the financial system.

The Canadian banking industry includes 20 domestic banks, 24 foreign bank subsidiaries and 22 foreign bank branches operating in Canada.

See also

- Banking in Canada
- List of banks in Canada
- List of Acts of Parliament of Canada

External links

- Canadian Department of Justice - Bank Act [2]
- Bank Act [3] at The Canadian Encyclopedia

Office of the Superintendent of Financial Institutions (Canada)

The **Office of the Superintendent of Financial Institutions** or **OSFI** is an independent agency of the Government of Canada reporting to the Minister of Finance created "to contribute to public confidence in the Canadian financial system". It is the sole regulator of banks, and the primary regulator of insurance companies, trust companies, loan companies and pension plans in Canada.

The current head of the Office is Julie Dickson, as of July 4, 2007. She replaced Nicholas Le Pan who resigned in July 2006. The term of the appointment is scheduled to be seven years.[1]

Mandate

The Office of the Superintendent of Financial Institutions (OSFI) was created to contribute to public confidence in the Canadian financial system.

OSFI's role is to:

- Supervise institutions and pension plans to determine whether they are in sound financial condition and meeting minimum plan funding requirements respectively, and are complying with their governing law and supervisory requirements;
- Promptly advise institutions and plans in the event there are material deficiencies and take or require management, boards or plan administrators to take necessary corrective measures expeditiously;
- Advance and administer a regulatory framework that promotes the adoption of policies and procedures designed to control and manage risk;
- Monitor and evaluate system-wide or sectoral issues that may impact institutions negatively.

OSFI's legislation has due regard to the need to allow institutions to compete effectively and take reasonable risks. The legislation also recognizes that management, boards of directors and plan administrators are ultimately responsible and that financial institutions and pension plans can fail.

The Office of the Chief Actuary, which is part of OSFI, provides actuarial services to the Government of Canada.

Related legislation

- Office of the Superintendent of Financial Institutions Act
- Bank Act
- Trust and Loan Companies Act
- Cooperative Credit Associations Act
- Insurance Companies Act
- Pension Benefits Standards Act, 1985 (PBSA)

History

Late 1800s – establishment of the Office of the Superintendent of Insurance (OSI), which subsequently became the Department of Insurance (DOI). The DOI was responsible for overseeing federally licensed life insurance companies, property and casualty insurance companies, trust and loan companies and pension plans, and for providing actuarial services to the government.

1925 – the Office of the Inspector General of Banks was established in response to the Home Bank failure and was responsible for regulating Canada's chartered banks.

Early 1930s – Royal Commission on Banking and Currency reviewed banking and currency issues in the Canadian financial system.

Early 1960s – Porter Royal Commission reviewed structural and operational issues affecting the financial system and financial institutions in Canada. The Commission's report concluded the financial system was sound, but developments had moved beyond the current state of laws and regulatory practices. Porter argued the public could not be insulated from loss in dealing with public institutions and markets. The Commission called for a system that would provide for adequate disclosure and that would set high standards of self-regulation, backed by strong government supervision and powers to enforce proper practices.

1967 – the Minister of Finance introduced legislation to establish the Canada Deposit Insurance Corporation (CDIC) to ensure the safety of small deposits and bring about a gradual improvement in the minimum financial standard of deposit-taking institutions in Canada. In 1983, legislative amendments extended CDIC's mandate to include assisting to maintain public confidence and stability in the financial system.

Mid-1980s – increased international competition and the failure of two Canadian banks and the subsequent enquiry into these failures by the Honourable Willard Z. Estey highlighted the need to ensure a sound approach to handling the risks associated with the financial marketplace.

July 1987 – to ensure a coordinated approach to supervision and a modern regulatory framework for Canada's financial system, and acting on the recommendations of the Estey commission, the government proclaimed the Financial Institutions and Deposit Insurance Amendment Act and the Office of the Superintendent of Financial Institutions Act. This latter Act joined the Department of Insurance and the Office of the Inspector General of Banks to form OSFI, which was given the powers to supervise and regulate all federally regulated financial institutions.

May 1996 – Bill C-15 receives Royal Assent. This new legislation clarifies OSFI's prime responsibilities as helping to minimize losses to depositors and shareholders, and contributing to public confidence in the Canadian financial system. Preventing failure of financial institutions is not part of OSFI's mandate; however, promoting sound business practices helps reduce the risk that financial institutions will fail. The mandate stresses the importance of early intervention to achieve OSFI's objectives and establishes the basis for OSFI's mission, objectives, priorities and strategies.

Sources

http://www.osfi-bsif.gc.ca/osfi/index_e.aspx?ArticleID=1534

See also

- Canada Deposit Insurance Corporation
- Banking in Canada
- Economy of Canada
- Canadian securities regulation

External links

- Office of the Superintendent of Financial Institutions web site [2]

Minister of Finance (Canada)

Minister of Finance

Ministry

Federal

Incumbent:
Jim Flaherty
PC, MP, BA, LLB
since 6 February 2006

Style:	The Honourable
Appointed by:	Michaëlle Jean as Governor General of Canada
First :	Alexander Galt
Formation:	1 July 1867
Term:	At Her Majesty's pleasure
Website:	www.fin.gc.ca [1]

Canada

This article is part of the series:
Politics and government of Canada

Other countries · Atlas
Politics of Canada portal

The **Minister of Finance** (French: *Ministre des Finances*) is the Minister of the Crown in the Canadian Cabinet who is responsible each year for presenting the federal government's budget. It is one of the most important positions in the Cabinet, and the Finance Minister must deal with all the other departments and plays an important role in deciding the funding levels for each.

The Minister of Finance is often one of the most unpopular positions in the government, being responsible at times for program cuts and tax increases. Paul Martin, however, seems to have overcome this and his long tenure as minister helped elevate him to the national popularity that allowed him to become Prime Minister. Martin was the fifth Prime Minister who was previously the finance minister; the others were Sir Charles Tupper, R.B. Bennett, John Turner, and Jean Chrétien.

The current Minister of Finance is Jim Flaherty.

Responsibilities

In addition to being the head of the Department of Finance, the Minister is also the government's lead in overseeing the:

- Bank of Canada
- Canada Deposit Insurance Corporation
- Canada Development Investment Corporation
- Canada Pension Plan Investment Board
- Canadian International Trade Tribunal
- Superintendent of Financial Institutions
- Financial Transactions and Reports Analysis Centre of Canada

Ministers

1.	Alexander Galt	July 1, 1867 - November 7, 1867	under Prime Minister John A. Macdonald
2.	Sir John Rose	November 18, 1867 - September 30, 1869	
3.	Sir Francis Hincks	October 9, 1869 - February 21, 1873	
4.	Leonard Tilley	February 22, 1873 - November 5, 1873	
5.	Richard John Cartwright	November 7, 1873 - October 16, 1878	under Prime Minister Alexander Mackenzie

	Sir Leonard Tilley *(2nd time)*	October 17, 1878 - November 11, 1885	under Prime Minister John A. Macdonald
	vacant	November 11, 1885 - December 10, 1885	
6.	Archibald McLelan	December 10, 1885 - January 27, 1887	
7.	Sir Charles Tupper	January 27, 1887 - May 22, 1888	
8.	George Foster	May 29, 1888 - June 6, 1891	
		June 16, 1891 - November 24, 1892	under Prime Minister John Joseph Caldwell Abbott
		December 5, 1892 - December 12, 1894	under Prime Minister John Sparrow David Thompson
		December 21, 1894 - January 6, 1896	under Prime Minister Mackenzie Bowell
*	Sir Mackenzie Bowell *(Acting)*	January 6, 1896 - January 15, 1896	
	George Foster *(2nd time)*	January 15, 1896 - April 27, 1896	
		May 1, 1896 - July 8, 1896	under Prime Minister Charles Tupper
	vacant	July 8, 1896 - July 20, 1896	under Prime Minister Wilfrid Laurier
9.	William Stevens Fielding	July 20, 1896 - October 6, 1911	
10.	Sir Thomas White	October 10, 1911 - August 2, 1919	under Prime Minister Robert Laird Borden
11.	Sir Henry Drayton	August 2, 1919 - July 10, 1920	
		July 10, 1920 - December 29, 1921	under Prime Minister Arthur Meighen
	William Stevens Fielding *(2nd time)*	December 29, 1921 - September 5, 1925	under Prime Minister William Lyon Mackenzie King
12.	James Robb	September 5, 1925 - June 29, 1926	
*	Sir Henry Drayton *(2nd time) (Acting)*	June 29, 1926 - July 13, 1926	under Prime Minister Arthur Meighen
13.	R. B. Bennett	July 13, 1926 - September 25, 1926	
	James Robb *(2nd time)*	September 25, 1926 - November 11, 1929	under Prime Minister William Lyon Mackenzie King
14.	Charles Dunning	November 26, 1929 - August 7, 1930	
	R. B. Bennett *(2nd time)*	August 7, 1930 - February 2, 1932	as PM
15.	Edgar Rhodes	February 3, 1932 - October 24, 1935	under Prime Minister R. B. Bennett

	Charles Dunning *(2nd time)*	October 24, 1935 - September 6, 1939	under Prime Minister William Lyon Mackenzie King
16.	James Ralston	September 6, 1939 - July 4, 1940	
17.	James Ilsley	July 8, 1940 - December 10, 1946	
18.	Douglas Abbott	December 10, 1946 - November 15, 1948	
		November 15, 1948 - June 30, 1954	under Prime Minister Louis Stephen St. Laurent
19.	Walter Harris	July 1, 1954 - June 21, 1957	
20.	Donald Fleming	June 21, 1957 - August 9, 1962	under Prime Minister John George Diefenbaker
21.	George Nowlan	August 9, 1962 - April 22, 1963	
22.	Walter L. Gordon	April 22, 1963 - November 11, 1965	under Prime Minister Lester Bowles Pearson
*	Mitchell Sharp *(Acting)*	November 11, 1965 - December 18, 1965	
23.	Mitchell Sharp	December 18, 1965 - April 20, 1968	
24.	Edgar Benson	April 20, 1968 - January 28, 1972	under Prime Minister Pierre Elliott Trudeau
25.	John Napier Turner	January 28, 1972 - September 10, 1975	
*	Bud Drury *(Acting)*	September 10, 1975 - September 26, 1975	
26.	Donald Stovel Macdonald	September 26, 1975 - September 16, 1977	
27.	Jean Chrétien	September 16, 1977 - June 4, 1979	
28.	John Crosbie	June 4, 1979 - March 3, 1980	under Prime Minister Joe Clark
29.	Allan MacEachen	March 3, 1980 - September 10, 1982	under Prime Minister Pierre Elliott Trudeau
30.	Marc Lalonde	September 10, 1982 - June 30, 1984	
		June 30, 1984 - September 17, 1984	under Prime Minister John Napier Turner
31.	Michael Wilson	September 17, 1984 - April 21, 1991	under Prime Minister Brian Mulroney
32.	Don Mazankowski	April 21, 1991 - June 25, 1993	
33.	Gilles Loiselle	June 25, 1993 - November 4, 1993	under Prime Minister Kim Campbell
34.	Paul Martin	November 4, 1993 - June 2, 2002	under Prime Minister Jean Chrétien
35.	John Manley	June 2, 2002 - December 12, 2003	
36.	Ralph Goodale	December 12, 2003 - February 6, 2006	under Prime Minister Paul Martin
37.	Jim Flaherty	February 6, 2006 - present	under Prime Minister Stephen Harper

Critics

- John McCallum 2006-present

See also

- Department of Finance
- New shoes on budget day (An unusual tradition among Ministers of Finance)

External links

- Department of Finance Canada [2]

Credit union

Financial market participants

- Collective investment schemes
- Credit unions
- Insurance companies
- Investment banks
- Pension funds
- Prime brokers
- Trusts

Finance series

- Financial market
- Participants
- Corporate finance
- Personal finance
- Public finance
- Banks and banking
- Financial regulation

A **credit union** is a cooperative financial institution that is owned and controlled by its members and operated for the purpose of promoting thrift, providing credit at reasonable rates, and providing other financial services to its members. Many credit unions exist to further community development or sustainable international development on a local level.

Worldwide, credit union systems vary significantly in terms of total system assets and average institution asset size, ranging from volunteer operations with a handful of members to institutions with several billion dollars in assets and hundreds of thousands of members. Yet credit unions are typically smaller than banks; for example, the average U.S. credit union has $93 million in assets, while the average U.S. bank has $1.53 billion, as of 2007.

The World Council of Credit Unions (WOCCU) defines credit unions as "not-for-profit cooperative institutions". In practice however, legal arrangements vary by jurisdiction. For example in Canada credit unions are regulated as for-profit institutions, and view their mandate as earning a reasonable profit to enhance services to members and ensure stable growth.

This difference in viewpoints reflects credit unions' unusual organizational structure, which attempts to solve the principal-agent problem by ensuring that the owners and the users of the institution are the same people. In any case, credit unions generally cannot accept donations and must be able to prosper in a competitive market economy.

Other names

In some places, credit unions are called by other names; for example, in many African countries they are called "savings and credit cooperative organizations" (SACCOs), "to emphasize savings before credit". in Spanish-speaking countries, they are often called *cooperativas de ahorro y crédito*, but in Mexico they are typically called a *caja popular*. French terms for "credit union" include *caisse populaire* and *banque populaire*. Afghan credit unions are called "Islamic investment and finance cooperatives" (IIFCs) and comply with Islamic banking practices.

Differences from other financial institutions

Credit unions differ from banks and other financial institutions in that the members who have accounts in the credit union are the owners of the credit union and they elect their board of directors in a democratic one-person-one-vote system regardless of the amount of money invested in the credit union.

A credit union's policies governing interest rates and other matters are set by a volunteer Board of Directors elected by and from the membership itself. Credit unions offer many of the same financial services as banks, often using a different terminology; common services include: share accounts (savings accounts), share draft accounts (checking accounts), credit cards, share term certificates (certificates of deposit), and online banking.

Normally, only a member of a credit union may deposit money with the credit union, or borrow money from it. As such, credit unions have historically marketed themselves as providing superior member service and being committed to helping members improve their financial health. In the microfinance context, "[c]redit unions provide a broader range of loan and savings products at a much cheaper cost [to their members] than do most microfinance institutions".

Global dispersion

The directors of the Mulukanoor Women's Thrift Cooperative stand at the entrance to their credit union in Warangal district, Andhra Pradesh, India

Based on data from the World Council of Credit Unions, at the end of 2006 there were 46,377 credit unions in 97 countries around the world. Collectively they served 172 million retail members and oversaw US $1.1 trillion in assets. Note that the World Council does not include data from co-operative banks, so that, for example, some nations generally seen as the pioneers of credit unionism, such as Germany, France, Netherlands and Italy, are not included in their data. The European Association of Co-operative Banks reported 34 million members in those four countries at the end of 2005.

The nations with the most credit union activity are highly diverse. According to the World Council, nations with the greatest number of credit union members included the United States (87 million), India (20 million), Canada (11 million), South Korea (4.7 million), Japan (3.6 million), Mexico (3.6 million), Australia (3.5 million), Kenya (3.3 million), Ireland (3.0 million), Thailand and Brazil (2.6 million each).

Countries with the highest percentage of members in the economically active population were Dominica (147% [numbers higher than 100% are possible because the average person is a member of more than one credit union]), Ireland (110%), Barbados (72%), Trinidad & Tobago (57%), Canada (48%), the United States (43%), Benin (27%), Australia (26%), Senegal and Mali (19% each).

History

Main article: History of credit unions

Modern credit union history dates to 1852, when Franz Hermann Schulze-Delitzsch consolidated the learning from two pilot projects, one in Eilenburg and the other in Delitzsch in Germany into what are generally recognized as the first credit unions in the world. He went on to develop a highly successful urban credit union system.

In 1864 Friedrich Wilhelm Raiffeisen founded the first rural credit union in Heddesdorf (now part of Neuwied) in Germany. Although Schulze-Delitzsch can claim chronological precedence, Raiffeisen is often viewed as more important today. Rural communities in Germany faced a far more severe shortage of financial institutions than the cities. They were viewed as unbankable because of very small, seasonal flows of cash and very limited human resources. The organizational methods Raiffeisen refined there, which levered what is today called social capital, have become a hallmark of the global credit union identity.

By the time of Raiffeisen's death in 1888, credit unions had spread to Italy, France, the Netherlands, England and Austria, among other nations. The Raiffeisen name is still used by Raiffeisenbank, the largest banking group in Austria (with subsidiaries throughout Central and Eastern Europe), Rabobank (Netherlands) and similarly named agricultural credit unions in Germany.

The first credit union in North America, the Caisse Populaire de Lévis in Quebec, Canada, began operations on January 23, 1901 with a ten cent deposit. Founder Alphonse Desjardins, a reporter in the Canadian parliament, was moved to take up his mission in 1897 when he learned of a Montrealer who had been ordered by the court to pay nearly $5,000 in interest on a loan of $150 from a moneylender. Drawing extensively on European precedents, Desjardins developed a unique parish-based model for Quebec: the *caisse populaire*.

In the United States, St. Mary's Bank Credit Union of Manchester, New Hampshire holds the distinction as the first credit union. Assisted by a personal visit from Desjardins, St. Mary's was founded by French-speaking immigrants to Manchester from Quebec on November 24, 1908. America's Credit Union Museum now occupies the location of the home from which St. Mary's Bank Credit Union first operated.

Pierre Jay, then Massachusetts Commissioner of Banks and Edward Filene, a Bostonian merchant, were central in establishing enabling legislation in Massachusetts in 1909. The Woman's Educational and Industrial Union, credited with many social service initiatives, heard of this cooperative financial model and wrote to DesJardins. He provided them with the data they needed and on November 23, 1910, they created Industrial Credit Union, the first non-faith-based or community credit union, established for all people in the greater Boston community. St. Mary's Credit Union (not to be confused with St. Mary's Bank Credit Union) was established in Marlborough, MA in 1913. Servicing any resident of the Commonwealth of Massachusetts, St. Mary's Credit Union is the oldest state-wide Credit Union nationally"St. Mary's Credit Union" [1]. Retrieved 2009-08-24..

Filene also created the Credit Union National Extension Bureau, the forerunner of the Credit Union National Association, which was formed as a confederation of state leagues at a meeting in Estes Park, Colorado in 1934. Attendees at the meeting included Dora Maxwell who would go on to help establish hundreds of credit unions and programs for the poor and Louise McCarren Herring, whose work to form credit unions and ensure their safe operation earned the title of "Mother of Credit Unions" in the United States.

In the same year, Congress passed the Federal Credit Union Act, which permitted credit unions to be organized anywhere in the United States. The legislation allowed credit unions to incorporate under either state or federal law, a system of dual chartering that persists today.

Not-for-profit status and the need for a surplus

In the credit union context, "not-for-profit" should not be confused with "non-profit" charities or similar organizations. Credit unions are "not-for-profit" because they operate to serve their members rather than to maximize profits. But unlike non-profit organizations, credit unions do not rely on donations, and are financial institutions that must turn what is, in economic terms, a small profit (i.e. "surplus") to be able to continue to serve their members. According to WOCCU, a credit union's revenues (from loans and investments) need to exceed its operating expenses and dividends (interest paid on deposits) in order to maintain capital and solvency and "credit unions use excess earnings to offer members more affordable loans, a higher return on savings, lower fees or new products and services".

WOCCU's position is deeply rooted in global credit union history. F.W. Raiffeisen, the founder of the global movement, wrote in 1870 that credit unions "are, according to paragraph eleven of the German law of cooperatives, "merchants" as defined by the common code of commerce. They accordingly form a sort of commercial business enterprise of which the owners are the [Credit] Unions' members".

Corporate credit unions

Most credit unions provide service only to individual consumers. By contrast, *corporate credit unions* (also known as *central credit unions* in Canada) provide service to credit unions, with operational support, funds clearing tasks, and product and service delivery. The largest corporate credit union in the United States is U.S. Central Credit Union of Lenexa, Kansas, which serves as a central clearing house for other corporate credit unions and holds approximately $45.3 billion in assets.

Leagues and associations

The World Council of Credit Unions is both a trade association for credit unions worldwide and a development agency. WOCCU's mission is to "assist its members and potential members to organize, expand, improve and integrate credit unions and related institutions as effective instruments for the economic and social development of all people".

Credit unions in the United States have traditionally used a state/national trade association relationship that aligns credit unions with state "Credit Union Leagues" followed by national affiliation with the Credit Union National Association (CUNA) of Madison, Wisconsin. Federal credit unions may also be members of the National Association of Federal Credit Unions (NAFCU).

The Credit Union Executives Society (CUES), based in Madison, Wisconsin, provides professional development and resources to thousands of credit union executives and directors worldwide. It partners with world-renowned universities to offer graduate-level executive education specifically for credit union leaders.

The biggest UK credit union trade association is the Association of British Credit Unions Limited, more commonly known as Association of British Credit Unions, ABCUL. A significant number of credit unions are affiliated to ACE Credit Union Services (ACECUS) or UK Credit Unions (UKCU). Many Scottish credit unions are represented by the Scottish League of Credit Unions (SLCU) which has headquarters in Glasgow; however the majority of larger credit unions choose ABCUL.

Credit Union Central of Canada is the trade association for Canada's credit unions outside Quebec. The Desjardins Group represents Quebec's credit unions. Structurally, it blends the functions of a trade association and a more European-style cooperative bank.

Credit Unions often form cooperatives among themselves to provide services to members. A Credit Union Service Organization (CUSO) is generally a for-profit subsidiary of one or more credit unions formed for this purpose. For example, CO-OP Financial Services, the largest credit union owned interbank network in the US, provides an ATM network and shared branching services to credit unions. Other examples of cooperatives among credit unions include credit counseling services as well as insurance and investment services.

In New Zealand, most credit unions are affiliated to the New Zealand Association of Credit Unions.

United Kingdom

Credit unions in the United Kingdom have a long history. Identical or similar institutions to the present-day credit union were known as mutual societies within the United Kingdom.

Institutions known as mutual societies grew out of the friendly society movement of the 18th century, with the first mutual insurer, Equitable Life, being founded in 1762. The emergence of mutual assurance was linked with the Industrial Revolution and the need to provide for impoverished workers beyond the outmoded Elizabethan Poor Laws, as people congregated in the cities and lived in conditions of squalor and poverty. The principle of mutuality goes back to this epoch, when the sophisticated financial institutions taken for granted today, did not exist.

The only method of improving the quality of ordinary people’s lives was through the development of co-operative and mutual societies, as formalised under the Friendly Societies Act 1819. Mutual institutions thus predated the welfare state and were formed to meet the needs of a burgeoning working class, consisting mainly of rural and immigrant workers. As a practical expression, this communitarian self-help movement allowed small regular individual contributions to be pooled for mutual collective benefit, obtaining the same economies of scope and scale necessary in providing collective insurance and banking products, to mitigate enduring social exclusion. Initially funding was required for housing, consumer durables and emergency insurance provision, at a time when commercial banks were still exclusively commercial lenders.

Building societies were formed as small temporary societies by worker co-operatives, pooling resources to build local houses and subsequently allocating them among members by drawing lots. Once all members were housed, these organisations were typically wound up, although some became permanent societies in an effort to promote wider home ownership, as exemplified by the Leeds Permanent Building Society, see. Surplus funds were then pooled, providing an opportunity for low-income families to earn interest on small deposits, with proceeds typically invested in residential mortgages and liquid government securities.

The traditional intermediation function of mutual societies was to promote thrift among the working classes and thereby provide access to low cost home loans. This ethos has become obscured in the recent battle for customers, and only the very real threat of extinction has occasioned any renewed vigour in proclaiming the original mutuality message. Mutual societies continue to perform vital social functions, often serving on the boards of local community groups, as well as regularly making sizeable local charitable donations. Indeed, the mutual legacy of social benefaction, although quite substantial, risks only being missed by the present generation once such institutions ultimately cease to exist. With the conversion of most of the larger remaining mutual societies into proprietary companies, the bulk of the UK savings assets will have shifted away from their traditional providers into the mainstream UK financial sector. This change is occurring even as the traditional barriers between banks, building societies and insurance companies are disappearing. The spate of conversions is leading to a polarisation into two camps: the converters and the remaining mutuals.

Credit unions in the United Kingdom have been regulated by the Financial Services Authority since July 2002. They are classified in two types: type 1 are the smaller credit unions while type 2 are larger. From November 2006 many type 2 credit unions began offering their members debit card accounts so that they could withdraw cash from any Link ATM.

In August 2010 the FSA will enact the CU-LRO (Credit Union - Legislative Reform Order) and widen access and modernise the powers of individual credit unions.

In October 2008 the Financial Services Compensation Scheme guaranteed the first 50,000 pounds of each saver's deposits in credit unions, in line with the guarantee for UK banks and building societies.

Credit unions in the UK now offer a wide range of services to their members; from direct debits to payroll deductions, from being able to send standing orders from their accounts to paying members bills to providing cheaper insurance facilities. Life insurance is usually included with membership (subject to pre-existing medical conditions and other exclusions). Death benefits vary between unions, but commonly include lump sum payments, writing off of outstanding loans and doubling of savings.

Credit unions offer savers considerably more protection than commercial "savings clubs", as was demonstrated by the 2006 collapse of the Christmas hamper club Farepak.

In June 2008, the Treasury announced plans to encourage the growth of credit unions by broadening the common bond and removing outdated restriction. The changes are intended to significantly reduce the influence of door step lenders and loan sharks.

Republic of Ireland

In June 2010, the Credit Union put forward plans to modernize the credit union.

Canada

Canada has the highest per-capita use of credit unions in North America, with more than a third of the population enrolled in one. They are popular in Quebec, where they are known as *caisses populaires* (people's banks).

As of December 31, 2007, the Caisses Populaires Desjardins federated 536 member caisses with CAD$ 144 billion in assets and 5.8 million retail members, making it the sixth largest financial institution in Canada.

Credit Union Central of Canada federates most credit unions in the English-speaking provinces. As of the end of 2009, the 10 affiliated systems operated 419 credit unions controlling CAD $122 billion in assets from 5.1 million retail members. In British Columbia, 46 credit unions with assets of $48 billion, serve 1.7 million people.

In Alberta, 46 independent credit unions, with 215 branches, serve more than 640,000 members. In Saskatchewan, 65 credit unions have 497,000 members and $12.2 billion in assets. Manitoba's 45 credit unions have 566,000 members with $14.6 billion in assets. In Ontario, 136 credit unions have 1.2 million members with $19.2 billion in assets. Major Canadian credit unions include Vancity (Vancouver), Coast Capital Savings (Surrey), Servus Credit Union (Edmonton), First Calgary Savings, Conexus (Regina), Meridian Credit Union (Ontario), Libro Financial Group (London, Ontario) and Credit Union Atlantic (Halifax).

United States

Main article: Credit unions in the United States

In the United States, as of 2005 credit unions have 86 million members, which is 43.47% of the economically active population. U.S. credit unions are not-for-profit, cooperative, tax-exempt organizations.

U.S. credit unions can be chartered by either the federal government ("federal credit unions") or by a state. The states of Delaware, South Dakota, and Wyoming do not regulate credit unions at the state level; in those states, a credit union must obtain a federal charter to operate. All federal credit unions and 95% of state-chartered credit unions have "share insurance" (deposit insurance) of at least $250,000 per member through the National Credit Union Share Insurance Fund (NCUSIF). This deposit insurance is backed by the full faith and credit of the United States government and is administered by the National Credit Union Administration. As of December 2006, the NCUSIF had a higher insurance fund capital ratio than the fund for the Federal Deposit Insurance Corporation (FDIC). U.S. credit unions also typically have higher equity capital ratios than U.S. banks.

As of April 2010, the world's largest credit union was Navy Federal Credit Union, serving U.S. Department of Defense employees, contractors, and families of servicepeople, with over $40.7 billion USD in assets and over 3.4 million members.

Industry trade organizations include the American Credit Union Mortgage Association.

See also

- Bond of association
- Cooperative
- Democratic member control (cooperatives)
- Friedrich Wilhelm Raiffeisen
- History of credit unions
- World Council of Credit Unions
- Consumers' cooperative

Further reading

- Ian MacPherson. *Hands Around the Globe: A History of the International Credit Union Movement and the Role and Development of the World Council of Credit Unions, Inc.* Horsdal & Schubart Publishers Ltd, 1999.
- F.W. Raiffeisen. *The Credit Unions.* Trans. by Konrad Engelmann. The Raiffeisen Printing and Publishing Company, Neuwid on the Rhine, Germany, 1970.
- Fountain, Wendell. *The Credit Union World.* AuthorHouse, Bloomington, Indiana, 2007. ISBN 978-1-4259-7006-2

External links

- World Council of Credit Unions [2] trade association for credit unions
- Association of Asian Confederations of Credit Unions [3] regional federation representing 21 national federations in Asia with 35 million retail members
- Credit Union Database [4] - All credit unions in USA
- Association of British Credit Unions Limited [5] - the largest trade body representing credit unions in the UK
- National Association of Credit Union Workers [6] - a staff association for all UK credit union workers regardless of trade body affiliation
- Scottish League of Credit Unions [7] - a trade body representing credit unions in Scotland
- ACE Credit Union Services [8] - a trade body representing many smaller credit unions in the UK
- UK Credit Unions [9] - a trade body representing many smaller credit unions in the UK

Article Sources and Contributors

Bank *Source*: http://en.wikipedia.org/?oldid=390307318 *Contributors*: 1 anonymous edits

Banking in Canada *Source*: http://en.wikipedia.org/?oldid=369344967 *Contributors*: Elsabaye

Early Canadian banking system *Source*: http://en.wikipedia.org/?oldid=360354445 *Contributors*: Victoriaedwards

List of banks and credit unions in Canada *Source*: http://en.wikipedia.org/?oldid=390185944 *Contributors*: 1 anonymous edits

British North America Acts *Source*: http://en.wikipedia.org/?oldid=389305736 *Contributors*:

Bank of Canada *Source*: http://en.wikipedia.org/?oldid=390438809 *Contributors*: 1 anonymous edits

Central bank *Source*: http://en.wikipedia.org/?oldid=390025615 *Contributors*:

Bank of Canada Building *Source*: http://en.wikipedia.org/?oldid=319171904 *Contributors*: Shawn in Montreal

Big Five (banks) *Source*: http://en.wikipedia.org/?oldid=385834227 *Contributors*: Raysonho

Royal Bank of Canada *Source*: http://en.wikipedia.org/?oldid=390260503 *Contributors*:

Toronto-Dominion Bank *Source*: http://en.wikipedia.org/?oldid=388073667 *Contributors*:

Scotiabank *Source*: http://en.wikipedia.org/?oldid=389550072 *Contributors*: 1 anonymous edits

Bank of Montreal *Source*: http://en.wikipedia.org/?oldid=390401926 *Contributors*:

Canadian Imperial Bank of Commerce *Source*: http://en.wikipedia.org/?oldid=390657812 *Contributors*: Koavf

National Bank of Canada *Source*: http://en.wikipedia.org/?oldid=385914905 *Contributors*: 1 anonymous edits

Desjardins Group *Source*: http://en.wikipedia.org/?oldid=378409506 *Contributors*: 1 anonymous edits

HSBC Bank Canada *Source*: http://en.wikipedia.org/?oldid=386923004 *Contributors*:

ING Group *Source*: http://en.wikipedia.org/?oldid=387206652 *Contributors*: 1 anonymous edits

Canada Bank Act *Source*: http://en.wikipedia.org/?oldid=387756495 *Contributors*:

Office of the Superintendent of Financial Institutions (Canada) *Source*: http://en.wikipedia.org/?oldid=386810272 *Contributors*: 1 anonymous edits

Minister of Finance (Canada) *Source*: http://en.wikipedia.org/?oldid=390518226 *Contributors*:

Credit union *Source*: http://en.wikipedia.org/?oldid=390630314 *Contributors*: 1 anonymous edits

Image Sources, Licenses and Contributors

Image:Cathay Bank Boston.jpg *Source*: http://en.wikipedia.org/w/index.php?title=File:Cathay_Bank_Boston.jpg *License*: Public Domain *Contributors*: Original uploader was HouseOfScandal at en.wikipedia

File:WinonaSavingsBankVault.JPG *Source*: http://en.wikipedia.org/w/index.php?title=File:WinonaSavingsBankVault.JPG *License*: Creative Commons Attribution-Sharealike 3.0 *Contributors*: User:Jonathunder

File:Halifax bank, Commercial Street, Leeds (27th May 2010).jpg *Source*: http://en.wikipedia.org/w/index.php?title=File:Halifax_bank,_Commercial_Street,_Leeds_(27th_May_2010).jpg *License*: unknown *Contributors*: -

File:NatWest Castle Street.jpg *Source*: http://en.wikipedia.org/w/index.php?title=File:NatWest_Castle_Street.jpg *License*: Attribution *Contributors*: Irate

File:ATM AL RAJHI BANK.JPG *Source*: http://en.wikipedia.org/w/index.php?title=File:ATM_AL_RAJHI_BANK.JPG *License*: Creative Commons Attribution 3.0 *Contributors*: haitham alfalah

Image:BBTLexington.jpg *Source*: http://en.wikipedia.org/w/index.php?title=File:BBTLexington.jpg *License*: Creative Commons Attribution 3.0 *Contributors*: User:Dennis Brown

Image:First Canadian Place.JPG *Source*: http://en.wikipedia.org/w/index.php?title=File:First_Canadian_Place.JPG *License*: unknown *Contributors*: -

Image:BankBritishNorthAmericaYonge23.jpg *Source*: http://en.wikipedia.org/w/index.php?title=File:BankBritishNorthAmericaYonge23.jpg *License*: unknown *Contributors*: -

Image:Red bar plain.png *Source*: http://en.wikipedia.org/w/index.php?title=File:Red_bar_plain.png *License*: GNU Free Documentation License *Contributors*: Athaenara, Jurema Oliveira, Skeezix1000

Image:BankofCanadabuilding.jpg *Source*: http://en.wikipedia.org/w/index.php?title=File:BankofCanadabuilding.jpg *License*: GNU Free Documentation License *Contributors*: User Peregrine981 on en.wikipedia

Image:London.bankofengland.arp.jpg *Source*: http://en.wikipedia.org/w/index.php?title=File:London.bankofengland.arp.jpg *License*: Public Domain *Contributors*: Adrian Pingstone

File:BankofCanadabuilding.jpg *Source*: http://en.wikipedia.org/w/index.php?title=File:BankofCanadabuilding.jpg *License*: GNU Free Documentation License *Contributors*: User Peregrine981 on en.wikipedia

File:Marriner S. Eccles Federal Reserve Board Building.jpg *Source*: http://en.wikipedia.org/w/index.php?title=File:Marriner_S._Eccles_Federal_Reserve_Board_Building.jpg *License*: unknown *Contributors*: -

Image:Bancocentralbrasil.JPG *Source*: http://en.wikipedia.org/w/index.php?title=File:Bancocentralbrasil.JPG *License*: unknown *Contributors*: -

File:BankIsrael01 ST 06.jpg *Source*: http://en.wikipedia.org/w/index.php?title=File:BankIsrael01_ST_06.jpg *License*: unknown *Contributors*: Mattes, Netanel h, ST, יבצ לאינד, 1 anonymous edits

Image:Royal Bank Building.jpg *Source*: http://en.wikipedia.org/w/index.php?title=File:Royal_Bank_Building.jpg *License*: Public Domain *Contributors*: Mortadelo2005, Skeezix1000, 1 anonymous edits

Image:Hwy404Hwy7RBC.jpg *Source*: http://en.wikipedia.org/w/index.php?title=File:Hwy404Hwy7RBC.jpg *License*: unknown *Contributors*: -

File:Rue stpierre.JPG *Source*: http://en.wikipedia.org/w/index.php?title=File:Rue_stpierre.JPG *License*: unknown *Contributors*: -

Image:2008-11-01 RBC Bank in Durham.jpg *Source*: http://en.wikipedia.org/w/index.php?title=File:2008-11-01_RBC_Bank_in_Durham.jpg *License*: unknown *Contributors*: -

Image:TD Centre View from Yonge and King.JPG *Source*: http://en.wikipedia.org/w/index.php?title=File:TD_Centre_View_from_Yonge_and_King.JPG *License*: unknown *Contributors*: -

Image:TDCTtower1.JPG *Source*: http://en.wikipedia.org/w/index.php?title=File:TDCTtower1.JPG *License*: Public Domain *Contributors*: User:Jxcacsijxcacsi

Image:Tdcommercebank.jpg *Source*: http://en.wikipedia.org/w/index.php?title=File:Tdcommercebank.jpg *License*: unknown *Contributors*: -

File:RegentStreetBZECITY.JPG *Source*: http://en.wikipedia.org/w/index.php?title=File:RegentStreetBZECITY.JPG *License*: unknown *Contributors*: -

Image:Toronto - ON - First Canadian Place.jpg *Source*: http://en.wikipedia.org/w/index.php?title=File:Toronto_-_ON_-_First_Canadian_Place.jpg *License*: GNU Free Documentation License *Contributors*: – Wladyslaw [Disk.]. Original uploader was Taxiarchos228 at de.wikipedia

File:Bank of Montreal building in Prince Rupert, British Columbia.jpg *Source*: http://en.wikipedia.org/w/index.php?title=File:Bank_of_Montreal_building_in_Prince_Rupert,_British_Columbia.jpg *License*: unknown *Contributors*: -

File:Bank_of_Montreal_branch_with_horse_and_carriage.jpg *Source*: http://en.wikipedia.org/w/index.php?title=File:Bank_of_Montreal_branch_with_horse_and_carriage.jpg *License*: unknown *Contributors*: -

File:Bank of Montreal 1 db.jpg *Source*: http://en.wikipedia.org/w/index.php?title=File:Bank_of_Montreal_1_db.jpg *License*: unknown *Contributors*: -

File:Bank of Montreal 4 db.jpg *Source*: http://en.wikipedia.org/w/index.php?title=File:Bank_of_Montreal_4_db.jpg *License*: unknown *Contributors*: -

File:St James Street, showing Bank of Montreal & Post Office, Montreal.JPG *Source*: http://en.wikipedia.org/w/index.php?title=File:St_James_Street,_showing_Bank_of_Montreal_&_Post_Office,_Montreal.JPG *License*: unknown *Contributors*: -

Image:BMO 3763.jpg *Source*: http://en.wikipedia.org/w/index.php?title=File:BMO_3763.jpg *License*: Public Domain *Contributors*: User:Myke2020

Image:Bank of Montreal 1 db.jpg *Source*: http://en.wikipedia.org/w/index.php?title=File:Bank_of_Montreal_1_db.jpg *License*: unknown *Contributors*: -

File:BankofCommerce1930.jpg *Source*: http://en.wikipedia.org/w/index.php?title=File:BankofCommerce1930.jpg *License*: unknown *Contributors*: -

File:Commerce Court.jpg *Source*: http://en.wikipedia.org/w/index.php?title=File:Commerce_Court.jpg *License*: unknown *Contributors*: -

Image:Desjardins Credit Union Toronto.jpg *Source*: http://en.wikipedia.org/w/index.php?title=File:Desjardins_Credit_Union_Toronto.jpg *License*: Public Domain *Contributors*: User:GTD Aquitaine

File:Flag of Canada.svg *Source*: http://en.wikipedia.org/w/index.php?title=File:Flag_of_Canada.svg *License*: unknown *Contributors*: -

Image:Hsbc-bldg.jpg *Source*: http://en.wikipedia.org/w/index.php?title=File:Hsbc-bldg.jpg *License*: unknown *Contributors*: -

File:HSBCMarkhamLibertySquare.jpg *Source*: http://en.wikipedia.org/w/index.php?title=File:HSBCMarkhamLibertySquare.jpg *License*: unknown *Contributors*: -

File:ING Group global locations.svg *Source*: http://en.wikipedia.org/w/index.php?title=File:ING_Group_global_locations.svg *License*: unknown *Contributors*: -

Image:INGHouse1.jpg *Source*: http://en.wikipedia.org/w/index.php?title=File:INGHouse1.jpg *License*: unknown *Contributors*: -

Image:Marquette Washington-20080925.jpg *Source*: http://en.wikipedia.org/w/index.php?title=File:Marquette_Washington-20080925.jpg *License*: unknown *Contributors*: -

Image:ING cafe 3d Av 58 jeh.jpg *Source*: http://en.wikipedia.org/w/index.php?title=File:ING_cafe_3d_Av_58_jeh.jpg *License*: unknown *Contributors*: -

Image:Ingdirectstcloud.jpg *Source*: http://en.wikipedia.org/w/index.php?title=File:Ingdirectstcloud.jpg *License*: Creative Commons Attribution 3.0 *Contributors*: User:Rtfagan

Image:ING London.png *Source*: http://en.wikipedia.org/w/index.php?title=File:ING_London.png *License*: unknown *Contributors*: -

Image:Large NYC MARATHON.jpg *Source*: http://en.wikipedia.org/w/index.php?title=File:Large_NYC_MARATHON.jpg *License*: unknown *Contributors*: -

File:Parliament-Ottawa.jpg *Source*: http://en.wikipedia.org/w/index.php?title=File:Parliament-Ottawa.jpg *License*: unknown *Contributors*: -

image:Jim Flaherty 2007.JPG *Source*: http://en.wikipedia.org/w/index.php?title=File:Jim_Flaherty_2007.JPG *License*: unknown *Contributors*: -

Image:Assorted United States coins.jpg *Source*: http://en.wikipedia.org/w/index.php?title=File:Assorted_United_States_coins.jpg *License*: unknown *Contributors*: -

file:Credit Union in Warangal, India.JPG *Source*: http://en.wikipedia.org/w/index.php?title=File:Credit_Union_in_Warangal,_India.JPG *License*: unknown *Contributors*: -

CPSIA information can be obtained
at www.ICGtesting.com
Printed in the USA
LVHW100821290521
688875LV00011B/694

9 781278 699981